"mine Angels round About"

Mormon Missionary Evacuation from Western Germany

1939

"mine Angels round About"

Mormon Missionary
Evacuation from
Western Germany

1939

Terry Bohle Montague

A portion of the proceeds from the sale of this title is donated
to the general missionary fund of The Church of Jesus Christ of
Latter-day Saints.

Distributed by:

PUBLISHING & DISTRIBUTION

Granite Publishing and Distribution, L.L.C.
868 North 1430 West • Orem, UT 84057
(801) 229-9023 • Toll Free (800) 574-5779
FAX (801) 229-1924

Production by: www.SunriseBooks.com

First edition 1989
ISBN: 1-878456-01-6
Library of Congress Card Number: 89-063510

Second edition 2000
ISBN: 1-930980-16-7

DEDICATION

This work is dedicated to my husband Quinn and my daughter Elizabeth, both of whom exhibited extraordinary patience with me as I researched, interviewed and traveled to many places in search of the missionaries whose experiences are recounted in this work. And to Norman Seibold whose story inspired its birth.

—*Terry Bohle Montague*

And whoso receiveth you, there I will be also, for I will go before your face. I will be on your right hand and on your left, and my Spirit shall be in your hearts, and mine angels round about you, to bear you up.

—*D&C 84:88*

TABLE OF CONTENTS

ACKNOWLEDGEMENTS

Among the many people and institutions to whom I am indebted in the completion of this project, I wish to especially note the following:

My husband and daughter, Quinn and Elizabeth Montague for their support. Former West German missionary, Owen Ken Earl, who prodded this project into shape and Susan Roylance of Roylance Publishing who believed in it.

The LDS Church Archives and Church Membership Office for their assistance.

The Twin Falls, Idaho and Cedar City, Utah high schools and the Alumni Associations of Brigham Young University, Idaho State University, Southern Utah State College, and the University of Utah for their assistance in helping locate many former West German missionaries.

Most especially, however, I would like to express my heartfelt gratitude and appreciation to those former West German missionaries and their families who have contributed to this project. They are: Donald Anderson, Grant W. Baker, Fredrick Balli, J. Richard Barnes, Calvin Bartholomew, George Blake, Sylvan Burgi, John W. Dean, Woodrow C. Dennett, Willard B. Doxey, Fred H. Duehlmeier, Bertha Raisch Duersch (widow of Nephi Henry Duersch and bookkeeper in the West German Mission office until 1939), Grace Olsen Ensign, Owen Ken Earl, Robert J. Gillespie, William George Goold, Whitney D. Hammond, Louis J. Haws, Arnold Hildebrandt, Clark M. Hillam, A. Burt Horsley, Liselotte Heitele Howell (widow of Geren Howell), Charles Jenkins Jr., Warren Kirk, Wesley P. Knudsen, Frank Knutti, Harold E. Kratzer, George P. Kuhn, Robert Kunkel, Claytor Larsen, Ben G. Lasrich, Joseph Loertscher, Howard W. Lyman, Fontella Blatter Maddox (sister of Leland Blatter), William R. Manning, Vern L. Marrott, Ferryle McOmber, Lawrence J. Meyer, Harry A. Niebuhr, Reed Oldroyd, Richard D. Poll, Ellis T. Rasmussen, Erma H. Rosenhan,

Elwood Scoville, Norman G. Seibold, Elmer E. Stettler, Lucille Goltz Stringham (daughter of Elizabeth and Adalbert Goltz), T. Frank Swallow, Douglas Niels Thompson, J. Ralph Thompson, Elmer Tueller, Dwayne Ward, George Wimmer, Wilford Woolf and Mission President M. Douglas Wood.

HOW THIS BOOK
CAME INTO BEING

Not long after my husband, Quinn, and I left Brigham Young University and moved to my hometown of Rupert, Idaho, Norman Seibold, a longtime resident and County Commissioner, spoke at a fireside in our Stake. His topic was his experiences as a missionary in Nazi Germany and his part in the West German Mission evacuation at the beginning of World War II, August 1939.

I approached Brother Seibold after his talk and suggested his story be recorded in detail. He thought the idea impractical since forty-five years had passed and he did not think he could remember enough of the details to put the entire story together.

I went to the Church Archives in Salt Lake City and was allowed into the West German Mission Journal.

I discovered Norman Seibold was not the only West German missionary to have had an adventure in getting out of Germany. Intrigued, I copied a list of all the missionaries serving in that mission in August of 1939 and began searching for each one.

That search took me two years. I found former West German missionaries in places as close as Burley, Idaho (only nine miles from my home) and as far away as New Zealand and Israel. I begged, cajoled and hounded most of those former missionaries into giving me their accounts of the evacuation. In the process, I collected four binders of correspondence, a suitcase full of tape recorded accounts, several hundred photographs and many, many treasured friendships.

The manuscript itself had a difficult birthing. The cast of more than eighty-five missionaries seemed Cecile B. DeMille size. Added to that, those eighty-five missionaries crisscrossed Germany, bouncing from border-to-border as they tried to get out of the country. Their experiences were as frantic and confused as the railway stations where most of the incidents occurred. For me, organizing the information into a readable story was frequently overwhelming and sometimes downright discouraging. So much so that at one point I filed the whole thing away and was prepared to leave it, suffering guilt pangs that could have registered on a seismograph.

Then in March 1989, Owen Ken Earl, an evacuated West German missionary, showed up at my home and said, "Let's get this thing out!"

The first edition of "mine angels round about" came out in November of 1989 and was sold out by the following February. I got involved in other writing projects and, though my husband urged me to push for another printing of "mine angels", I felt I was too busy.

For ten years I got phone calls from people looking for copies. I was always sorry to say there were none. Then, oddly, in 1999 and 2000, I began getting at least a phone call every week from someone who wanted a copy of "mine angels round about". We decided it was time for another printing.

I must say I am a better writer now than I was in 1989. I spent a month re-writing the "mine angels" manuscript. So while this is only a second printing, it is a revised printing. It doesn't read exactly as the first printing but the story is still as dynamic and uplifting and still bears testimony that the Lord truly does protect and care for his missionaries.

—Prologue—

1938-1939

1938. The bleak decade of the thirties drew to a close. In the United States, Franklin D. Roosevelt's New Deal began to restore his countrymen's faith in themselves and promised a brighter, more prosperous future.

At the same time, rumors of civil unrest and war spread across the face of the earth. In India, the "skinny man", Mohandas K. Gandhi, campaigned for passive resistance against Great Britain. The ongoing bloody dispute between Japan and Russia spread to China. Ecuador fought with Peru over boundary territory, and Spain fought with itself.

Europe, its wounds barely healed from the Great War, was still recovering from an economic depression, when it faced a new threat. The menacing growth of Nazism in Germany.

Dictator, Adolph Hitler, claimed the Jews' control of European economics caused Germany's defeat in the previous war. And he insisted the devastating depression which had followed was the result of the Versailles Peace Treaty of 1918. The Treaty, he declared, thieved hundreds of square miles of German border territory.

Hitler promised the German people the return of that territory. He promised the Fatherland would be reborn in strength and vigor and pride. He would annihilate the Jews and tear up the Peace Treaty. The embittered German people rallied to his support with wild enthusiasm.

In defiance of the Treaty, Hitler reintroduced the draft to Germany and built an army of half a million men. Then, the Germans marched into and again occupied the Rhineland, a strip of land along the French border. France, fearing a confrontation, stood

President and Sister Wood rollerskating in Frankfurt

unprotesting in the face of Germany's aggression.

Despite the threat of war, The Church of Jesus Christ of Latter-day Saints continued to send their missionaries into Germany. That year, the growing Swiss-German Mission was divided and M. Douglas Wood became President of the newly created West German Mission.[1]

President Wood, an energetic young man, was scarcely older than many of the missionaries over whom he was called to preside. Dark-haired, he wore a thin, dapper mustache popular in the thirties. His wife, Evelyn, later to become known through her Reading Dynamics Program, was a clever young woman for whom the missionaries developed a warm regard. "Mission Mother" was not a term frequently applied to Sister Wood. More often she was called the "Mission Sweetheart".[2]

West German Mission Home in Frankfurt 1939

In March 1938, Nazi Germany annexed Austria and gained six million new countrymen.

During the following summer, Hitler turned an avaricious eye toward Czechoslovakia. He demanded the return of a strip of land along the German-Czech border known as the Sudetenland.

Eduard Daladier, the French Premiere, warned the Nazi government if Germany attacked Czechoslovakia, France would declare war on Germany.

Great Britain's Prime Minister, Neville Chamberlain, hesitated to join Daladier in issuing the warning. He believed peace could be kept by giving Germany what it wanted.

The Czechs bravely resisted as Germany increased its demands. The French Army and British Navy mobilized. The Czechs stood ready to fight.

In the East and West German Missions, the missionaries were ordered to evacuate to Rotterdam, Holland.

Some missionaries were unconcerned about their ordered exodus from Germany. "We'll be back," they assured the German members.

The members, however, viewed the evacuation with alarm. They believed that losing the missionaries meant abandonment by the Church. For many branches, consisting mostly of women and small children, the missionaries were their

American Flag flanked by swastikas at the Romerberg in Frankfurt on 30 May 1939

Europe in 1939
including some cities of
the West German Mission.

only priesthood authority. Without them, the German Saints could not receive the sacrament. Also, the missionaries served as branch presidents, Sunday School presidents and Primary presidents.

A great concern was that the German members' link to LDS Church Headquarters and the Prophet, Heber J. Grant, would be severed. Without the guidance of the Prophet and the General Authorities of the Church, the members feared the collapse of the Church organization in Germany.

But the most frightening aspect of an evacuation was the indication that the Prophet believed Germany was unsafe for the missionaries. For German members, who believed Heber J. Grant received direct inspiration and revelation from God, that indication was clear evidence of an approaching conflict. Many Latter-day Saints wept with fear at the departure of the missionaries. They remembered too well the horrors of a war only a generation past.[3]

Anthony Woolfe remembered one particular member who was not so much frightened by the missionaries' evacuation as she was outraged by their abandonment. "Coward," she called Woolfe and insisted the missionaries were "running away."

Chamberlain and Daladier rushed to Munich for conferences with Hitler. The Fuhrer argued, threatened, bullied and bamboozled the two leaders into believing war was an instrument solely in his power. If his demands were not met, he would use that instrument.

The English and French leaders were willing to do almost anything to avoid another war. Even if the peace was kept at the expense of the Czechs. Chamberlain and Daladier handed the Sudetenland over to Hitler.

At 1:00 a.m. on September 30 1938, Adolph Hitler, Benito Mussolini, Neville Chamberlain and Eduard Daladier signed the Munich Agreement.

Overwhelmed with relief, a grateful Europe heard Chamberlain declare, "The peace has been preserved!"

The signing of the Agreement also meant the missionaries could return to Germany. The members would be relieved. Or so thought missionary Clark Hillam.

In early October 1938 when Hillam and his companion returned from Holland to Saarbruecken in southwest Germany, their reception was not what they had anticipated.

One of their first visits took them to a Brother Kieffer in his camera shop. The two missionaries were shocked by the older man's appearance. He was pale and much thinner than when they had seen him only a month earlier.

You should have never come back," he declared.

Kieffer told them this story: Several months earlier, a missionary named Adams[4] who was assigned to Saarbruecken, came into his camera shop and asked Kieffer to develop a roll of film. Among the pictures on the film was one in which Adams and his companion had the flag of the Third Reich draped around them.

Soon after, Adams and his companion were transferred to separate cities. When the companion asked for a copy of the picture, Adams took the negative to another camera shop for a reproduction. The proprietor asked to see the original photograph. Adams produced it. The man turned over the photo, and, discovering Kieffer's stamp on it, called the police. Kieffer was arrested. The police accused him of treason. They insisted he was using the LDS missionaries as operatives in a spy ring.[5]

Kieffer denied the charges. They had no proof, he protested, other than a photo taken by two indiscreet young Americans. They could not accuse him of a serious offense on such flimsy evidence.

Perhaps not, the interrogators replied. However, they intended to hold him while they sought other evidence which would support a charge of treason.

Kieffer was put in a concentration camp but was released when the charges could not be proved. After his release, Nazi officials kept a watchful eye on him, his family, his home and his business.

"The police know everywhere you go and everything you do," he told Hillam. "You should not be here!"

Shaken, Hillam and his companion rode their bicycles twenty-five miles to a neighboring town and telephoned the mission office in Frankfurt.

President Wood immediately transferred the pair.[6]

Woodrow Dennett told about an experience when he was not as cautious as the situation required.

> In Stuttgart we had a little joke. Each radio station had its own call tone. One of the missionaries came up with a little ditty to go with the chimes of one of the call tones. It went "Der Fuhrer iss une dummerkarel." (The Fuhrer is a stupid fellow.)
>
> One morning, I came downstairs in the house where we were living and the radio was on. Without thinking, I sang, "Der Fuhrer iss une dummerkarel." A little girl who lived there heard me. I didn't know she was there. She took it to school and the teacher heard her and sent her to the principal.
>
> When she came home that day I was at Primary but my companion, Fred Duehlmeier was there. When he heard about what had happened, he came over to the Primary meeting and asked, "Did you do that?"
>
> I said, "I believe I did."
>
> He said, "How could you be so dumb? You'd better get to that school just as fast as you can get there."
>
> He took over Primary and I went to the school. I talked to the principal and he didn't mince any words.
>
> He said, "It's a good thing you came in and explained. The police station is on my way home and I was going to stop in there. I know where you would have been in a week!"[7]

In November 1938, Herschel Grynszpan, a seventeen-year-old German-Jewish refugee, was living in Paris. His father was one of 10,000 Jews rounded up by the Gestapo and deported from Germany to Poland in box cars. On November 7, shortly after the incident, an enraged Grynszpan went to the German Embassy in Paris. At the gate, the young man demanded to see the German Ambassador, Count Johannes von Welczeck. The guard, suspicious of the wild-eyed youth, alerted the ambassador.

Count von Welczeck sent this third secretary, Ernst von Rath, into the yard. Mistaking von Rath for the ambassador, Grynszpan raised his revolver and fired.

German doctors rushed to Paris to treat von Rath.

Ironically, the wounded secretary did not share the anti-semitic attitude embraced by the Nazi party. For weeks, the Gestapo had been following von Rath and documenting his movements.

Some Church members confided to the missionaries their belief that if von Rath's wounds were not fatal, the Nazi-controlled physicians would see that they became so.[8]

In Munich on November 9, the Nazi Party held its annual anniversary celebration of the 1923 Beer Hall Putsch. The party bosses, led by Hitler and Hermann Goering, paraded through the city's streets. In the Munich Stadium, a vast assembly of tanks and trucks formed huge displays of strength for the gathered thousands. Goose-stepping, column upon column of uniformed soldiers marched into the arena. Bombers and fighter planes filled the skies.

In his speech before this enormous audience, Hitler warned the outside world not to interfere with Germany or its people. The crowd roared its approval.

That evening, began a horror which has come to be called the Week of Broken Glass.

Dr. Paul Joseph Goebbles, a small man sometimes called the "poison dwarf", held the post of Propaganda Minister. He bragged that the larger the lie, the more likely it was to be believed. Goebbles intended a colossal lie for that evening.

Goebbles organized "spontaneous demonstrations" directed against the Jews of Germany. He intended the "demonstrations" look like an outraged, spontaneous uprising in retaliation for von Rath's murder.

It was obvious, however, to Germans as well as the American missionaries that the people who were involved in the "demonstrations" were members of the Schutzstaffel, the dreaded SS, in civilian clothing.

That night, called "Crystal Night" for the smashed glass sparkling in the gutters, members of the SS broke into, looted and burned synagogues, Jewish hospitals, shops and homes. Some Jews, including women and children, were slain as they tried to escape being burned to death.

In horror, many missionaries watched as the SS beat and molested men, women and children and destroyed their property. Donald Anderson witnessed the stoning of Jewish business men in front of their shops and stores.[9]

Similar scenes were repeated across Germany. Two missionaries awakened by a red glow reflected on the walls of their apartment, raced to the window and saw the synagogue across the street engulfed in flames. They dressed quickly and joined the crowd outside their building.

At that moment, looters pushed a grand piano from a fifth floor landing of the synagogue. It crashed to the cobblestone street below and shattered into hundreds of pieces.

"This is terrible. This is terrible," muttered an elderly German who stood next to the missionaries in the watching crowd. "If they do this to the Jews, who will be next? Who will stop them from doing this to anyone else?"[10]

The Week of Broken Glass was Arnold Hildebrandt's introduction to Germany. When he arrived in the city of Gera, the railway station was crowded with wretched looking prisoners. Dirty and caked with mud, men, women and children huddled and squatted on the platforms, their knees under their chins, their faces a reflection of shock and despair.

Having just come from Milwaukee, Wisconsin, and knowing nothing whatever about Jews or the anti-semitic attitude of the Nazi government, Hildebrandt was puzzled.

"Who are these people?" he asked his landlady who had come to meet him at the railroad station. The woman shook her head and with a gesture instructed him to be silent. Later, she told Hildebrandt to forget what he had seen in the train depot.[11]

Norman Seibold also remembered an incident in the Nuremburg railway station. Idly, Seibold walked up and down the platform as he waited for his train. A commotion at the other end of the station drew his attention. Armed guards stood with their rifles leveled as Jews of all ages climbed from the cattle cars of one train and filed across the yard to another. Their heads had recently been shaved. As they passed Seibold, he saw many still had blood crusted on their scalps where the razor had nicked their skin.

Helpless, Seibold turned away.[12]

In Augsburg, Grant Baker and William George Goold noticed a huge plume of black smoke rising above the house tops. They hurried through the streets and discovered a Jewish hospital in flames. A fire truck stood by in case any surrounding building should also catch fire. But the firemen made no move to extinguish the blaze.

Patients who were able to do so tried to escape the burning building. Some dragged and pushed their beds into the street.

Discreetly, the missionaries snapped pictures of the scene, then left the area as unobtrusively as possible. They took the film to the shop of a German friend whom they believed they could trust. When the shop's proprietor saw what was on the film, he called the police.

The officers came for Baker and Goold the following day. They took them to a nearby police station and interrogated them for several hours. Then they escorted the thoroughly frightened young men back to their apartment.

In silence, the pair watched the police search their closet, clothes, dresser drawers, trunks and beds. They even inserted long, thin metal probes into their straw-tick mattresses in an effort to discover evidence which would prove the missionaries were subversives or spies.

The officers confiscated church records as well as the missionaries' passports, personal papers and journals. Then, they ordered the missionaries into the street and a waiting car. The police drove them into the countryside and described in lengthy and gruesome detail the concentration camp in nearby Dachau.

At last, satisfied that they had adequately impressed the two young Americans, the officers returned them to their rooms.

For the next three weeks, Baker and Goold were under constant surveillance. They knew their rooms were being watched. They were also aware of the car that shadowed them through Augsburg's streets. When the driver of the vehicle realized the missionaries knew he was following them, he merely drove along beside them as they walked.

During those weeks, the pair attempted, in vain, to recover the records and personal property the police had confiscated. The local branch president, Hans Thaller, also appealed to the police at some risk to himself. However, he met with a similar lack of success.

Desperate, the missionaries went to the American Consulate in Munich but the Consul refused to intervene for them.

After a month, the police returned the items to the missionaries and President Wood transferred Baker and Goold to other cities.

Upon his arrival in Bremen, Goold was not surprised when the local police appeared at his door and demanded he turn over his passport and personal papers. When the policeman left, Goold went to the consulate in Bremen to protest the action. Again, the Consul refused to become involved.

It was nearly a month later when the police returned Goold's passport.[13]

The Nazi government kept a cautious eye on the religious activities of the German people. "We want no God but Germany!" Hitler declared. Books supporting Christian ideals and principles were publicly burned in huge bonfires.

On a more subtle level, Hitler had plans for the Catholic Church in which he held membership. "I'll have my reckoning with the Church," he declared, referring to the priests and nuns as "black crows". "I'll have it reeling on the ropes!"

Hitler disbanded the Catholic Youth Association and replaced it with his own organization, the Hitler Youth. At the age of ten years, boys of the organization swore the following oath:

> In the presence of this blood banner, which represents our Fuhrer, I swear to devote all my energies and strength to the Savior of our country, Adolph Hitler. I am ready and willing to give up my life for him, so help me God.

Activities for Hitler's youth, as well as political rallies, were scheduled on Sundays to discourage children and their parents from attending church services.[14]

Hitler also demanded Protestant ministers swear a loyalty oath to him. In fear of their lives, many complied. Those who did not—nearly a thousand of them—were arrested and put in concentration camps.

The LDS Church did not escape the notice of the Nazi officials. "You blunt the intellects of the people!" an official told one branch president.[15]

Members and missionaries were constantly warned by their Church leaders to be circumspect in their actions and avoid voicing opinions that were contrary to government policies. Even the West German Mission Journal includes no mention of the strain that existed between the Church and the State—with one exception.

An entry made during the early part of 1939 states President Wood reproved an unnamed missionary for his vocal opposition to the Nazi government. The young man was threatened with immediate release from his mission if he persisted. The journal recorded no other details.

Although the winter of 1938-39 passed quietly, tension in the West German Mission grew. The Nazi government ordered the missionaries to sign statements agreeing they would not go from home to home or be involved in any group discussions in any park or on the streets. Only Sunday meetings were allowed. But those were often interrupted by the arrival of SS officers, who silently watched the congregation from the back of the room. Any other special meeting had to be approved by the local police.[16]

Government interference was obvious in nearly every aspect of the missionaries' daily lives. Even their letters from home were opened and read by censors before they were delivered. Portions of the letters, judged inappropriate by officials, were cut out of the pages.

Harry Niebuhr said a friend mailed him several sticks of chewing gum. When he got them, it was obvious from the condition of the wrappers, the gum had been opened and inspected.[17]

Despite these conditions, the missionaries persevered. They joined clubs and groups, even organizations connected with Hitler's Youth, to meet people and introduce them to the Gospel.

They participated in sports events, gave athletic exhibitions, taught classes and formed musical groups. They also relied on cottage meetings in the homes of church members. The missionaries found, however, members and contacts were so anxious about the possibility of war, they would not discuss anything else.

In March 1939, Hitler was successful in gaining the return of Memel, a German city which had been ceded to the tiny country of Lithuania by the Versailles Peace Treaty.

Full of confidence, Hitler then turned his attention to the city of Danzig. The Treaty had ceded that city to Poland, but the Nazis demanded its return, too. Hitler also demanded free access to East Prussia across the narrow strip of Polish territory called the Danzig Corridor.

Poland, a long time foe of Russia and defiantly anticommunist, had sought a friendship with Germany in the early days of Hitler's reign. That friendship began to sour, however, with the Fuhrer's increasing demands.

On March 15, Nazi troops marched into Czechoslovakia and, despite the promises in the Munich Agreement, took that country in a bloodless coup.

Wimmer, Baker, Thompson, Hillam, Alder, Knudsen, Earl, Jenkins

*Fitz Duehimeier (Number 8) joined the German police against a
Finnish Team in June 1938*

Poland awakened that morning to find itself flanked, not only
by the despised Russians on the east, but the German Army on the
south and west.

Enraged by Hitler's double-dealing in Czechoslovakia, Great
Britain and France declared they would lend Poland all the support
in their power. Throughout that spring, Poland steadfastly refused
German demands and resisted Hitler's threats.

Of that time, George Blake wrote:

> All during the summer of 1939, missionaries in Germany
> heard strange bits and pieces of news indicating a heightening
> political crisis. Signs that should have been clear and indeed
> alarming in their implications seemed to come and go but were
> passed over [in] the day to day missionary life. We had seen the
> building of the fortified 'West Wall' along the upper Rhine
> Valley during the spring and summer. In June we saw a twenty-
> three plane armada, a large aggregation at that time, heading
> eastward. A few days later, cavalry passed our window all night
> long. One of our friends in the Party's women's auxiliary told us
> early in July there would be a showdown over the Danzig
> Corridor shortly. And we heard that the farm leaders had been
> ordered to get the wheat harvest completed by August 10. Yet

with such indications and more, we simply couldn't internalize the truth that a serious crisis was approaching. Certainly, it would be no more than a skirmish, a temporary dislocation in our missionary activities."[18]

Indeed, missionaries observed many indications of the approaching crisis. The Versailles Peace Treaty limited Germany to an army of no more than 100,000 men. The navy was restricted to six ships and an air force was strictly prohibited. Yet the missionaries witnessed daily displays of the Treaty's violations.

Ships were being built and launched in the northern port city of Kiel. Nearly a million men received their draft notices. Automobile manufacturing plants turned out military vehicles instead of cars. In small city airports, an unusual number of pilots were being trained and it was rumored that not far from the Polish border, thousands of men worked day and night on a new airfield.[19]

Through the summer, it was reported 70,000 Germans from the Danzig Corridor fled to Germany. The refugees told harrowing tales of Polish brutality. According to their accounts, German women and children were being murdered by the Poles.

Under the direction of Dr. Goebbles, camera crews filmed the refugees as they told their stories. The films, intended to arouse sympathy from the Germany people and whip up a frenzy of war

Typical farming scene in 1939

fever, were shown in theaters across the country and used as evidence for the need of military intervention in Poland.

Toward the end of summer, fresh fruits, vegetables and meat became increasingly scarce. Early in the morning, as soon as it was light, long lines formed at the markets.[20]

In the bakeries, bread was made from a poor grade of flour that was extended with sawdust. More than one missionary picked splinters of wood from his teeth after eating the unsavory bread.[21]

Many missionaries lived on a daily diet of fish and potatoes, a more than adequate fare by German standards.[22]

The Fuhrer disdained meat and alcohol, preferring simple, inexpensive foods. He expected the German people to live by that same standard. And with the threat of war in Poland, he declared it to be the duty of patriotic Germans to cut down on food by serving a one-dish meal—usually soup—on Sundays. The money they saved on food for that day was to be contributed to a fund for guns and ammunition.

On August 8, there was a rumor of an agreement between Germany and Russia. The rumor suggested the two countries would sign a pact and then divide Poland between them.

The West German missionaries watched with a growing sense of apprehension. Again, Mission President Wood cautioned them to be ready at any time to evacuate to Holland.[23]

On August 10, the newspapers carried bold banners. "DANZIG OR WAR!" On the radio that night, Hermann Goering declared, "We do not need eggs and butter. We need guns!"

Fighter planes and bombers filled the skies over Mainz on August 11. The newspapers reported more violent attacks on German citizens by Poles.[24]

On August 17, William Manning recorded:

> Some of our members who were in the German Army told us that some of their units stationed in Bielefeld were leaving for the Polish border tonight. There was nothing in the newspaper about it.[25]

What the newspaper did declare was, "1,000 Germans in Polish Prison! Murders and Persecutions on Reichdeutche in Polish Territory!"

In the city of Weimar, during the early hours of August 20, companions Ellis T. Rasmussen and Frank Knutti were awakened by the rumbling of traffic from the cobblestone streets below their apartment. A long column of trucks, tanks and uniformed soldiers passed through the town for more than twenty-four hours. All were moving north toward the Polish border.[26]

The blackouts began on August 21. The order mandated that lights were to be extinguished or covered after dark to shield troop movement.

Leland Blatter recorded this on August 21:

> Had a talk with our mailman this morning and he is surprised that we are still here. He says things are not looking so good. I noticed they had taken another large number of men from town here. Teaching is almost impossible. The first thing they say is, "What do you think? Will we have a war or not?" You can't get anyone to talk about the gospel as they are all scared stiff that they will soon be fighting again. I don't blame them. It does look bad.[27]

On August 22, the end for Poland was in sight. Newspapers reported a non-aggression pact signed between Russia and Germany.

In the mission office, President Wood and his staff prepared for the arrival of Apostle Joseph Fielding Smith and his wife, Jessie Evans.

Smith was coming to Germany to conduct missionary conferences in fourteen cities. The tour, beginning in the northern German city of Kiel, would end in Vienna, Austria.[28]

President and Sister Wood, who were to make the tour with the Smiths, asked Arnold Hildebrandt to accompany them as they traveled to Kiel and act as translator for the Apostle. The five boarded the train in Frankfurt during the evening of August 21 and arrived in Kiel on the 22nd.

Two days later, on the morning of August 24, J. Richard Barnes, secretary of the West German Mission, received a telephone call in the Frankfurt office. "Dick," the caller said, "this is President Brown." Then Hugh B. Brown, President of the British Mission, told Barnes he had just received a telephone call from the First Presidency in Salt Lake City.

Because they were unable to get through to Germany by telephone, they had contacted President Brown and asked him to relay a message to the mission offices of the East and West German Missions. The message from President Heber J. Grant was, "In three days, the German Army will invade Poland."

This was followed by instructions for getting word to Apostle Smith and two other important American church members who were traveling in central Europe. Instructions were also given for evacuating all U.S. missionaries into Holland and Denmark.

Barnes wrote:

> I immediately contacted President Wood and Apostle Smith in the Schleswig Holstein portion of northern Germany. They instructed me to immediately contact each of our missionaries by telephone and give them evacuation instructions.
>
> I first went to the U.S. Consul General in Frankfurt, with whom I had an excellent relationship. I informed him of the message from President Grant. I then asked him to get on his coded wire to the Military attache in the U.S.Embassy in Berlin and ask him what knowledge he had on German military buildup or movement.
>
> The response from Berlin was, "There is no indication of any German military buildup or movement."
>
> The Consul General then said to me, "Mr. Barnes, if our Military Attache' has no knowledge of such activity on the part of the Nazi Army, from what source is your church President getting the information?"
>
> My answer was, "I know he got the information from the Lord." We then had a brief discussion about the calling of the President and Prophet of the Church.
>
> He said, "I have to believe that is the source of his information."[29]

ENDNOTES

1 West German Mission Journal is kept in the LDS Church Archives in Salt Lake City, Utah. A mission journal is a journal kept by the mission president's secretary. It chronicles the events of the mission office.

2 Bertha Raisch Duersch personal interview. Mrs. Duersch was a German member of the Church who served as the bookkeeper in the mission office until 1939.

3 Clark Hillam personal interview.

4 The name Adams is a fictitious one. Clark Hillam was the first to contribute this account but it was later substantiated by two other former West German missionaries.

5 In Nazi Germany, the traditional sentence for treason was beheading with an axe.

6 Hillam interview.

7 Woodrow Dennett personal interview.

8 An interesting sidelight about Grynszpan is that although he was arrested and charged with murder by the French and later turned over to the Nazis, he was never tried. According to Who's Who in Nazi Germany by Robert Wistrich (Bonanza Books 1982), Goebbles planned a sensationalistic trial in 1942 in which the boy would not only be convicted of murder, but the Jewish people, as a whole, would be blamed as the cause of the war between Germany and France.

    Then, an anonymous letter to the German authorities claimed Grynszpan and von Rath were homosexual lovers. Wishing to avoid a possible scandal, Goebbles abandoned plans for the trial. Because Grynszpan was held in a Berlin jail until the end of the war, he escaped being sent to a concentration camp. Wistrich claimed Grynszpan changed his name and, by last account in 1957, was living in Paris.

9 Donald Anderson written account.

10 Tape recording made by Vern Marrott.

11 Tape recording made by Arnold Hildebrandt.

12 Norman Seibold personal interview.

13 William George Goold and Grant Baker accounts.

14 William George Goold and Joseph Loertscher accounts.
15 West German Mission Journal.
16 Joseph Loertscher and Reed Oldroyd accounts.
17 Harry Neibuhr personal interview.
18 George R. Blake written account.
19 Anderson account.
20 Marrott account.
21 Niebuhr account.
22 Charles Jenkins Jr. written account.
23 William R. Manning written account.
24 Marrott account
25 Manning account
26 Frank Knutti personal interview.
27 Leland Blatter's missionary journal was provided by his sister, Fontella Blatter Maddox.
28 Hildebrandt account.
29 J. Richard Barnes made the wry comment that President Heber J. Grant had a better source of intelligence than the U.S. military.

Below are the names of the West German missionaries on the following page:

1st row: Warren P. Kirk, Rolland H. Rose, Willard B. Doxey, Reed Oldroyd, George Kuhn, Louis J. Haws, J. Richard Barnes, Richard E. J. Frandsen, Owen Ken Earl, Wesley F. Knudsen, Darrell S. Robins, Elmer R. Tueller, Whitney D. Hammond, Sylvan Burgi, Myron Seamons.

2nd row: Lydia Heibel, Elfriede Marach, Ilse Kramer, Katharine Riegler, Nikolaus Riegler, R. Keith Parker, Calvin Bartholomew, Vern L. Marrott, Evelyn N. Wood, President M. Douglas Wood, George R. Blake, A. Burt Horsley, Ilse Brunger, Nephi H. Duersch, Wilford Wegener, Grant A. Brown, June Hickman (Swiss), Wilford W. Woolf

3rd row: Weldon M. Mathis, Erma Rosenhan, Grace Olsen, Hildegard Heimburg, Elwood Scoville, Donald Petty, H. Christian Pieper, T. Paxman Martin, Geren B. Howell, Harold E.. Kratzer, Don B. Gubler, John W. Dean, Osmond L. Harline, Robert Kunkel, Earl M. Fuhriman, Clark M. Hillam, R. Larkin Glade.

4th row: Woodrow C.Dennett, Grant W. Baker, Grant W. Weber, Norman Seibold, Ellis T. Rasmussen, Paul S. Nicholes, Douglas Thompson, Arnold Hildebrandt, Claytor Larsen, Shirl H.Swenson, Frank Knutti, Emil Fetzer, Horace G. Moser, Clarence Beuhner, George Goold, Joseph Wirthlin (Swiss), Lawrence J. Meyer, Edward Wirthlin.

5th row: Donald R. Anderson, T. Frank Swallow, H. Clive Kimball, Albert Beutler (Swiss), Alfred W. Alder, John H. Wells, Ferryle McOmber, Dwayne D. Ward, Ben C. Lasrich, Edward Mabey, Harry Niebuhr, Eugene S. Hilton, Leland B. Blatter, Ernest Stettler, Robert James Gillespie, Vernon Sorenson.

6th row: Doris E. Black, Erich W. Bauer, Fred H. Duehlmeier, L. John Bingham, George A. Wimmer, J. Ralph Thompson, Stanford Poulson, Dean G. Griner, Howard W. Lyman.

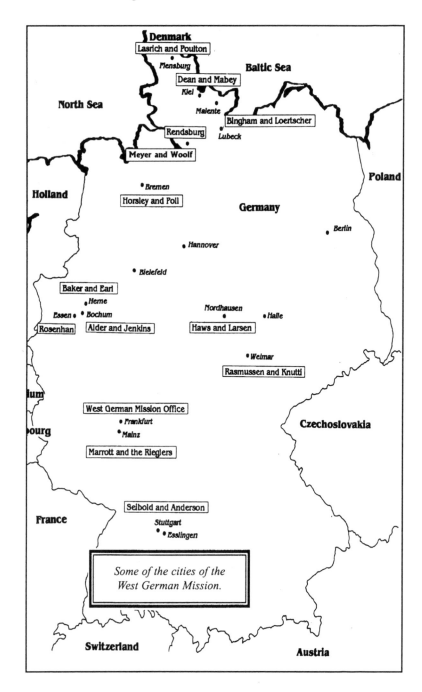

*Some of the cities of the
West German Mission.*

—ONE—

FRIDAY, 25 AUGUST 1939

"Leave immediately for Rotterdam"

The Mission Office in Frankfurt

In Hanover, during the early morning of August 25, Joseph Fielding Smith told President and Sister Wood and Arnold Hildebrandt that a telegram had come from the First Presidency instructing all American missionaries to be evacuated to either Holland or Denmark.

West German Mission Office Staff, Summer 1939
Front: Barnes, Anna Wood, Kramer, Harline
Middle: Tueller, Kimball, Heimberg, The Woods, Frandsen, Hildebrandt
Back: Scoville, Weber, Hammond

The evacuation orders meant immediate action. The missionaries had to be notified, Church records as well as personal belongings had to be packed and, in some cities, entire branches must be reorganized. There was a great deal to be done and little time to see it all accomplished. President Wood had to return to the mission office as quickly as possible.

The trip from Hanover to Frankfurt took six hours by train, but the urgency of the situation demanded a much faster method of travel. Wood went to the hotel clerk and asked him to call the airport for tickets. The clerk was skeptical. He told Wood reservations must be made weeks in advance. And with all available aircraft being diverted to the Polish border, he could see no possible way airline tickets could be secured.

"Call them for us anyway," Wood insisted. "We must have two reservations."

Minutes later a baffled hotel clerk reported to President Wood, "There are two reservations left."

Leaving Hildebrandt to escort the Smiths to Frankfurt by train, the Woods boarded the plane and were in Frankfurt an hour and twenty minutes later. That flight was the last passenger service flight before the plane was sent from Frankfurt east to the Polish border.

At the mission office, Wood telephoned the Dutch Consul. Since Holland was more centrally located in relation to the West German Mission and since the evacuation in 1938 took the missionaries to that country, it was decided the missionaries should again be evacuated to Holland. Wood asked permission for the missionaries to take refuge there, the Consul granted the request and the evacuation telegrams went out.

> Leave immediately for Rotterdam. Trunks same train. Appoint temporary successor. Wire Quickmere upon departure. Wood.

Hours passed. Despite instructions that the missionaries wire the code word "Quickmere" as they left their assigned cities, the mission office staff received no word from any of them.

President Wood became more and more concerned. He puzzled over the matter and two explanations presented themselves. Either the missionaries' departure telegrams with the code word "Quickmere" were not being delivered to the mission office or, he thought with a sinking heart, the missionaries did not receive the telegrams instructing them to evacuate.

"We'll have to try to telephone," he said.

Only a few missionaries had access to telephones. To reach them, the mission staff would have to telephone the post offices in the various cities where the missionaries were assigned. The post office would then send a courier to the missionaries rooms with a message instructing them to call the mission office. The missionaries would have to go to the post office to make the return call.

It was a long shot—too long.

After many frustrating delays in the telephone service, an operator broke in. "The lines are tied up with priority military calls," she told them. The mission office would not be able to complete their calls.

There was one other alternative, but barely that.

President Wood instructed his secretary, J. Richard Barnes, to try wiring a second telegram to the missionaries.

Barnes called the telegraph office but the operator told him the wires had been temporarily closed to all but priority messages.

There was nothing left to do but wait and pray the first telegrams would, somehow, be delivered.[1]

In Bremen

Richard D. Poll's journal entry for August 25 reads, "Today had no ending; it went right into tomorrow."[2]

Poll, a wavy-haired Texan from Fort Worth, and his companion, A. Burt Horsley, bicycled seventy-five miles to attend the Hanover Conference on August 24. They heard addresses from Apostle Smith, President and Sister Wood and listened as Sister Smith, a soloist with the Mormon Tabernacle choir, sang.

Unaware that an evacuation was being planned, the two missionaries returned to Bremen on the 25th, again cycling the seventy-five miles.

Bone-weary after the long ride, the pair arrived at their apartment at 7:30 p.m. Within moments, the telegram arrived.

"Leave immediately for Rotterdam..."

It was late when they finished packing and sat down to take stock of their funds. Poll had recently received money from home and, since it was illegal to take more than 10 Reichmarks (about $2.50) out of Germany, they decided to spend what they had on souvenirs.

Every West German missionary dreamed of owning the high quality photography equipment produced in Germany. It was with this in mind that the pair set out to find a shop where they could buy the items they wanted.

Unfortunately, it was well after the regular hours kept by the city's stores and shops. Their landlady, however, knew the proprietor of a drug store who was willing to sell them what they wanted. There was one hitch.

Because of the blackout order, the shop owner refused to turn on the lights in his store. He gave the two young men flashlights and told them they had to keep the beams from being seen in the street. He insisted they crawl on their hands and knees through the dark store until they found the equipment they wished to buy.

The missionaries wired "Quickmere" to the mission office, left their bicycles with their landlord and boarded the 12:15 a.m. train for Holland.[3]

In Herne and Bochum

In the city of Herne in Westfallen, Owen Ken Earl, from Bunkerville, Nevada, had just returned to his room and was preparing a talk for Sunday. His companion, Grant Baker and two other missionaries, Charles Jenkins Jr. and Alfred Alder had gone to the public bathhouse.[4]

About 6:00 p.m. the missionaries' landlady, Frau Jollenbeck, heard Earl cough and came to his door with a telegram. He opened it, looked at it and, at first, thought it was in German. He handed it back to Frau Jollenbeck, who also tried to read it but could not. Then Earl looked at it more closely and realized that, although it was written in German script, the message was in English.

"Leave immediately for Rotterdam…"

Earl rushed out, leaving an alarmed Frau Jollenbeck standing in his room. His companion, Grant Baker and Alfred Alder and Charles Jenkins, Jr. had already left the baths. By the time Earl returned to their room, Baker was there but Alder and Jenkins were on their way back to their rooms in Bochum.

Earl showed the telegram to Baker who rushed after Alder and Jenkins.

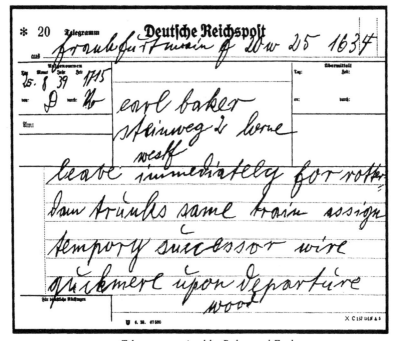

Telegram received by Baker and Earl

Grant Baker and Ken Earl say good-bye to the Uhlstein family.
This is the last known photograph of Herbert Uhlstein.
He was killed in combat shortly after it was taken.

During the rest of the day and part of that night all four missionaries prepared to leave. Laundry had to be picked up, Branch records moved to local Church headquarters and belongings packed.[5]

While picking up their laundry at Sister Rutrecht's home, through her tears, she repeatedly told Earl, "Immer lachen, Bruder Ken. Immer lachen." (Always smile, Brother Ken. Always smile.)

In Bochum, Jenkins set off to the post office to mail some letters. Jenkins had been in Germany only a few weeks but thought he would have no difficulty with a short trip to the post office. He found he was wrong.

Unaware he was going the wrong way, Jenkins entered a one-way street. A policeman stopped him and lectured him briefly. Being unfamiliar with the language, Jenkins got back on his bicycle and proceeded down the street—still going the wrong direction.

The policeman stopped him again. Upon discovering the missionary spoke no German, the officer arrested Jenkins took him to the police station. His passport was confiscated, and he was accused of being a Polish spy. A serious charge.

Even though Jenkins passport identified him as an American citizen, police officials remained suspicious. But despite his inability to speak the language, Jenkins was, at last, able to convince them he was not a spy.

The police returned his passport and released Jenkins who, by then, was a shaken but more cautious young man.[6]

In Stuttgart

On that same Friday, Norman Seibold and Donald Anderson noticed the streets of Stuttgart were unusually crowded. All capable military personnel had been ordered to report to their units that day. Everywhere there were soldiers.

Seibold reported feeling an unnatural undercurrent of emotion in the people on the street—unrest, anxiety and fear.

When the pair returned to their apartment, they found a letter from the American Consul in Stuttgart advising them to leave Germany.

> It has been learned that in view of the present tension in Europe, the American Embassy in Berlin is advising American citizens that it might be best to leave Germany.
>
> This advice, of course, does not imply that the Embassy or any Consular Office can assume any responsibility in connection therewith, but each one who may act upon this suggestion or advice must do so at his own risk and responsibility.[7]

Having no word from President Wood, the missionaries laid the letter aside and prepared to retire.

Later that night, Geren Howell, a missionary from the neighboring town of Feuerbach, burst into their apartment. Howell said he and his companion had just received a telegram from the mission office.

"Leave immediately for Rotterdam…"

Seibold rose, dressed and went to the local post office where there was a telephone. He called the mission office in Frankfurt and spoke to President Wood. The president explained the situation and instructed Seibold to go to the town of Esslingen the following morning and see that Adalbert and Elizabeth Goltz, an elderly missionary couple, were ready to go.[8]

In Mainz

In mid-July, Vern Marrott, a soft-spoken young man from Pleasant Grove, Utah had been assigned not one new companion but two. Nikolaus and Katharina Riegler. Riegler and his wife were German converts to the Church. They had immigrated to the United States and raised their family in Utah. Then in their retirement years, they received a mission call to Germany with the specific assignment to return to their hometown of Mannheim and contact family and friends about the Church.

But when the Reiglers were transferred to Mainz, they were unhappy. They felt they should be in Mannheim. They wanted to go back.

Marrott did his best to convince the couple to stay and work with him. He stressed the importance of the work they were called to perform in Mainz. At last, with great reluctance, the couple agreed to remain. But Marrott knew they were still homesick for Mannheim.

Then Sister Riegler became ill. She suffered from a chronic stomach ailment that seemed to be relieved only by a daily diet of six fresh eggs and a quarter pound of butter. Of all the rationed food in Germany, eggs and butter were the most scarce. Since butter was rationed to one-eighth pound per person per week, Marrott asked the members in Mainz to sacrifice their rations to help Sister Riegler.

The problems did not end there, however. In her discomfort, Sister Riegler was inclined to complain about the food their land-lady, Frau Burkehardt, prepared for them. Frau Burkehardt reacted by flatly refusing to do any further cooking and cleaning for the missionaries. Those tasks were left for Marrott.

Even more discouraging for the young missionary was that all their proselyting efforts in Mainz had come to a standstill. No one wanted to discuss the gospel. All the talk was of Poland and the possibility of war. With every new political rumor, the Rieglers threatened to leave Mainz and go back to Mannheim.

On that Friday afternoon, Marrott and the Rieglers attended a cottage meeting and returned late to their apartment. Since it was still light, Marrott suggested they sit in the quiet park near their apartment for a while. At first, the Rieglers declined. Brother Riegler had been ill a few days earlier and still complained he did not feel well.

"It may be our last chance," Marrott said, thinking the fresh air would do them good.

At that moment from down the street, Walter, the fourteen-year old son of their landlady, came running toward the trio with a mes-sage in his hand.

"Call office, 61967, immediately. Wood."

The three missionaries knew what it meant. Marrott told the Rieglers to return to their rooms and pack. Then he and Walter ran to the post office to telephone Frankfurt.

After several unsuccessful attempts, the telephone operator broke in and told Marrott there was no point in continuing his efforts. The lines were jammed with priority military calls.

Marrott decided the only way to find out the details of President Wood's message was to catch a train from Mainz to Frankfurt, a distance of about forty miles.

The Frankfurt railway depot was in chaos. Uniformed soldiers, headed east to Poland, crowded onto the platforms while Jews and foreigners formed long lines at the ticket offices. Baggage handlers, frenzied under the pressure of the added work load, shouted obscenities as they wildly heaved, tossed and threw trunks, suitcases, crates and boxes onto the train.

In the mission office, Marrott could see his suspicions about an evacuation were correct. Open, half-packed trunks and suitcases lined the hallways. The desks stood with their drawers gaping as the staff frantically rushed between desks and trunks.

J. Richard Barnes showed Marrott his shorthand of President Grant's telegram ordering the mission evacuated. He told Marrott to return to Mainz, pack as quickly as possible and head to Holland.

It was after midnight when Marrott's return train pulled into Mainz. He found the wild scene from the Frankfurt station being reenacted there. Everywhere soldiers milled, paced and checked and rechecked train schedules. Some stood in silent, solemn clumps, smoking cigarettes. Another group formed a ring around two soldiers in a bloody fight.

Since the missionaries would need a baggage handler to come to their apartment for their trunks, Marrott approached the baggage master who was barking at his overwrought and over-worked staff. It took some persistence to get the baggage master's attention. He agreed to send a man for the trunks as soon as possible.

Then Marrott went to the railway ticket office to buy three tickets to Rotterdam. As in Frankfurt, the office was besieged by foreigners and German Jews attempting to leave Germany. Marrott waited in a thirty minute line to make his purchase.

When he returned to the apartment, Marrott found the Rieglers in the middle of packing. He gathered his own belongings and crammed them into his trunk. Dawn was just streaking the sky when he finished packing. Then he sat down and wrote goodbye letters and cards to the members of the Mainz Branch.

It was 5:30 a.m. when a weary Vern Marrott crawled into bed.[9]

In Weimer

It was 8:00 p.m. in the city of Weimar. Ellis T. Rasmussen, a lean, blond young man, and his companion from Salt Lake City, Frank Knutti, heard a commotion in the street below their apartment.

"Herr Rasmussen! Herr Rasmussen!" someone was shouting.

Rasmussen went to the window and called down to the uniformed courier, "I am Herr Rasmussen."

The man waved a piece of paper up at him saying, "I have a telegram for you."

"Leave immediately for Rotterdam…"

The missionaries went straight to their landlady. An exacting woman, she had locked the missionaries' luggage in her attic to discourage any thought they might have of slipping out without paying the rent.[10]

She allowed the two young men to haul their trunks from her attic. They spent the rest of the evening packing their belongings.

Then Rasmussen telephoned Karl Woolfe, a member of the Weimar Branch, and explained they had been instructed to leave the country.

Despite the late hour, Woolfe offered to drive them and their luggage to the railway station.

With little time to spare before the departure of the midnight train, they appointed and set apart Woolfe as president of the branch. They gave him the branch records and asked him to give their bicycles to needy members. Then they sent a telegram to the mission office with the code word "Quickmere", loaded their trunks into Woolfe's car and sped to the train depot.

They were ten minutes too late for the midnight train.

The pair dropped down on a bench inside a shelter on the station platform and wondered what to do next. They rechecked the train schedule and discovered another train, leaving within a few minutes, was headed northeast to the city of Halle.

Halle was in the wrong direction but they reasoned, from there they could catch a train headed west to the Dutch border.[11]

Eight Missionaries on a Holiday

The sun shone down on nine bicyclists as they peddled the winding forest roads through Schlesig Holstein in picturesque northern Germany. Although the skies were clear, the air was heavy with a humidity that heralds a coming storm.

The missionaries had attended the mission conference held in Kiel and afterward received permission from President Wood to bicycle through the popular tourist area.

Eight of the nine were West German missionaries. John W. Dean, a veteran missionary assigned to Kiel, came from Heber City, Utah. He introduced many young men to the gospel by organizing and coaching basketball teams. His companion was Edward Milo Mabey, a giant of a young man.[12]

John Bingham and Joseph Loertscher were assigned to Lubeck. Bingham was due to be released in a few weeks while Loertscher, from the sleepy town of Huntington, Utah, had just arrived.[13]

Donald Poulton and Ben Lasrich were assigned to the German-Danish border city of Flensburg. Lasrich, an affable, young man, was the son a German couple who settled in Salt Lake City after their conversion.[14]

Salt Laker Lawrence J. Meyer, another veteran missionary assigned to Rendsburg, his companion Wilford Woolf and Hienie Kuhn, a young German member from Kiel, made up the balance of the group.[15]

An unusual incident, a sharp reminder of the ever-present threat, marred what had been a pleasurable day.

Loertsher wrote:

> After passing through some forest area and around the lakes, we came to a large dike which stretched for several blocks. On top of the dike was a barbed wire fence. We could hear unusual

noises coming from the other side. We climbed the dike and looking over, were surprised to see several large fields filled with military equipment and soldiers marching everywhere. What was so strange was the fact they had long picks and shovels over their shoulder for weapons. It did not take us long to leave that area.[16]

As the day ended, the nine pitched their tents and borrowed arms-full of straw from a local farmer and laid their bed rolls on it. Unfortunately, the straw was full of hungry insects and following an unpleasant night, the young men rose early the next morning.[17]

Over a somber breakfast, Bingham and Loertscher decided to return to Lubeck instead of continuing the trip.[18]

The remaining young men spent the Friday cycling through the forests, as well as swimming and sailing on one of the many lakes. After sunset, they put up their tents and rode into the city of Malente for dinner. While there, the missionaries heard government officials had ordered all resort hotels in the area vacated to quarter in-coming troops. The rumor numbered them in the thousands.

The missionaries were aware Germany had been fortifying itself for war. That possibility, however, had always seemed remote. With the information that thousands of soldiers would be moving into the area, so close to the Polish border, they knew the war everyone predicted and dreaded was at hand.

Alarmed, the missionaries raced back to their tents, packed their belongings and rushed to a nearby railway station. They reasoned that if there was word of a missionary evacuation, it would be at the apartment of John Dean and Edward Mabey in nearby Kiel.

In Kiel, Lasrich, Poulton, Meyer and Wilford Woolf waited on the street while Dean and Mabey ran upstairs to their room.[19]

"Leave immediately for Rotterdam…"

Lasrich and Poulton raced to the railway station where they hoped to catch a train to Flensburg, their assigned city on the Danish border.

There were no scheduled trains, however, and with no other alternative, they hired a taxi cab to take them the fifty miles from Kiel to Flensburg.

They had gone barely a mile and were still in the city when their taxi was involved in an accident. The vehicle was badly smashed and people were coming from all directions. Lasrich and Poulton knew the police would be on the scene at any moment. They knew they would be involved in a lengthy investigation. They knew they couldn't afford any more time. In the confusion of the moment, the missionaries slipped out of the taxi and hurried down several streets until they found another cab.

They arrived in Flensburg at midnight and packed until 4:00 a.m. Then they collected their laundry, sent a telegram to the mission office with the code work "Quickmere" and visited some of the members to say goodbye.

"They cried for fear as we left," Lasrich recorded in his journal.[20]

A Sister in Essen

In Essen that Friday evening, August 25, Erma Rosenhan and her German companion, Lydia Heibel, were at the home of Brother and Sister Paul Kuepper. At 8:30 p.m., Else Biehl, the branch president's sister, came to the door. She told Sister Rosenhan word had come from President Wood that the First Presidency had ordered all American missionaries to leave German immediately.

Sister Rosenhan's heart sank.

Born in the United States to German parents, Erma's Patriarchal Blessing stated her people needed the genealogical work she could do for them. Along with the desire to fulfill a mission, she hoped her call would be to Germany. In that way, she would be able to serve in the county of her parent's birth and perhaps have access to the genealogical records she needed.

Unfortunately, the prevalent circumstances of that time seemed to thwart the tall, willowy girl at every turn.

Nearly everyone suffered financial difficulties during the 1930's and Erma's family was no exception. For a long time they did not have the money to help support a missionary.

When the money was, at last, available, the Church announced it would no longer call sister missionaries to strife-torn Europe.

In patience and faith, Erma waited. Then, a close female friend was called on a mission to Berlin. Erma went to Harold G. Reynolds, Church Mission Secretary and listed all the reasons she should serve a mission to Germany.

"I shouldn't give too much of an argument," he said when she finished.

Erma was called to the West German Mission.

She was in the Salt Lake City Mission Home during the autumn of 1938 when the West German missionaries evacuated to Holland. And, despite rumors of an impending war and the Czechoslovakian crisis which sent the missionaries headlong out of Germany, there was never any doubt in Erma's mind. She would serve her mission in Germany.

The crisis over, Erma arrived in Germany in late October 1938. She was assigned to Lydia Heibel, a companion who would become her lifelong friend.

To research her family history, Erma hired a genealogist. Only eight days earlier, he had mailed her all the information he had gathered. Now it looked as though that information could not have come any later.

Erma and Lydia left the Kueppers and went to the home of Branch President Walter Biehl who had managed to contact the mission office by telephone.

He had been told a missionary was on his way to Essen to see Erma safely out of the county. She must be ready to leave when he arrived.

Biehl also took that opportunity to give Erma an unusual but inspired piece of counsel. He told her to buy a ticket to London instead of Rotterdam. Erma realized if she was to have a ticket to London, she would also need a British visa.

Kuepper took her into town on the back of his motorcycle. They stopped first at the railway station. A train was leaving at 8:04 the following morning. Then she and Kuepper rode to the British Consulate for a visa but found the dark building locked and seemingly abandoned. Upon investigation, they learned the British Consul had left Germany two weeks earlier and no one knew where his representative lived.

They went to the police station to have Erma's passport stamped. An officer told her the necessary stamp was locked up for the night. She would have to return at 7:30 a.m. to have her passport validated.

Undaunted, Erma declared that when her missionary escort came for her, she was leaving whether her passport was stamped or not.

The policeman objected. She would not be allowed to cross the border without the appropriate stamp on her papers.

"Our Prophet has told us we have to go and I have to follow my Prophet," she insisted.

At her apartment, Erma quickly packed. The minutes and hours of that night passed. But no missionary arrived for her. She laid down on the bed and tried to rest but feared falling asleep. Up again, she paced the floor, frequently going to the window and looking up and down the dark street.

At about 2:00 a.m., Erma noticed lights coming on in the apartments starting at the end of the street. A figure was going from door to door. By the time the man came to her apartment building, she recognized the mail carrier.

Cheerfully, he called to her from the street, "Fraulein, it is late. Why are you still up?"

"I'm getting ready to leave Germany," she answered.

"You needn't go," he replied, teasing lightly. "Things are not as bad as that."

"They are bad enough that the President of my Church has ordered all the American missionaries to leave."

The man sobered. He told her he was out that night delivering military summons for those required to report to their units that same day. He was to report on the second military call. The man was silent for a moment, then added, sadly, "I leave two children at home."[21]

Joseph Fielding Smith on the Dutch Border

During the evening of Friday, August 25, Apostle Joseph Fielding and Jesse Evans Smith left the headquarters of the West German Mission in Frankfurt and traveled by train to the Dutch border. To the Smiths' great surprise, the border officials refused to allow them to enter the country.

The officer explained that during the last war, neutral Holland was overrun by refugees from nearly every county in Europe. The subsequent food shortages had been devastating to the small county. The residents had starved. With war again brewing in neighboring Germany, Holland had closed its doors to all refugees.

Smith protested. They were not refugees. He was there to set up temporary headquarters for the American LDS missionaries who were being evacuated from all parts of Germany. The Dutch Consul had given permission for them to come to Holland.

Unsympathetic, the officials answered roughly that they knew nothing of the Dutch Consul. Their orders were to turn back all refugees.

Smith gave them his guarantee. The missionaries would not become a burden to the Dutch Government. The Church would assume full responsibility for them while they were in Holland. The officials remain adamant. No refugees. No exceptions.

Grimly, Apostle Smith thought of the eighty-four missionaries who were, at that moment, on their way to the Dutch border. What was to become of them?[22]

ENDNOTES

1 Wood, M. Douglas. "The Lord Stood at Our Side." *Deseret News* Church Section, 15 June 1940.

2 Richard Poll personal interview.

3 Poll interview.

4 Many German households did not have bathing facilities. The West German missionaries used public bath houses.

5 Owen Ken Earl journal.

6 Charles Jenkins Jr. account.

7 Many former West German missionaries felt the American Consulates in Germany did not advise Americans to leave the country until it was learned the Mormon missionaries were being evacuated.

8 Norman Seibold interview and Donald Anderson tape.

9 Vern Marrott tape.

10 Frank Knutti tells this interesting story about their landlady: The day before the missionaries received the evacuation telegram, their landlady left Weimar by train to visit her sister in another city. She was to have been gone for several weeks. While the landlady was on the train, she became so ill she decided to return to Weimar.

   Knutti noted that had she not returned, he and Rasmussen would have had to leave without their luggage—an upsetting thought for those whose families had to struggle to provide the necessary funds for mission clothing.

11 Frank Knutti interview. Rasmussen, Ellis T. "Border Incident, Inside Germany," *Improvement Era.* (December 1943. pp 793-4.)

12 Brigadier General John W. Dean written account.

13 Joseph Loertscher written account.

14 Ben Lasrich mission journal.

15 Lawrence J. Meyer letter.

16 Loertscher account.

17 Lasrich mission journal.

18 Erma Rosenhan letter.

19 Dean account and Lasrich mission journal.
20 Lasrich mission journal.
21 Erma Rosenhan letter
22 Smith, Joseph Fielding. "Border Incident," *The Improvement Era*, (Dec. 1943, p.752)

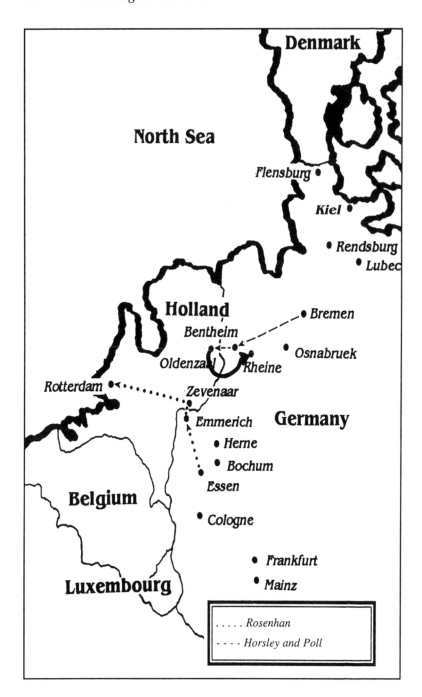

—TWO—

SATURDAY, 26 AUGUST 1939

On the Way to Holland

Leland Blatter

Leland Blatter recorded in his journal:

> August 26, 1939. We visited as many of our friends and
> members as we could. It was hard to leave. Some of the old
> members wept and wished they could go with us. I also wished I
> was able to take them. It was hard leaving them after they had
> been so good to us. But we had to go.[1]

Erma Rosenhan

Erma Rosenhan waited and watched through the long night but
the missionary who was supposed to come for her did not arrive. It
was 5:00 a.m. There was a train leaving Essen at 8:04 that morning
and, even if it meant going alone, Erma knew she could wait no
longer. The local district president, Walter Biehl, and his brothers
came to her apartment with a hand cart and loaded her luggage on
it. Then she, her companion Lydia Heibel and the Biehls, walked to
the Essen-West railway depot pushing the loaded cart. At the station they were told Erma's trunks could not be checked onto the
train at that depot—she would have to take them across the city to
the main railway station.

Although the distance was not too far to walk, little time remained for all that had to be done, so Biehl called for a taxi.

When the cab arrived, the driver was willing to take the passengers into Essen but refused to take the trunk. He claimed the added weight burned too much gasoline. All the available fuel had been allocated to the military that day and the cab had been rationed a few liters. After that was gone there would be no more.

After a lengthy argument, the driver agreed to take the trunk. They loaded the luggage into the taxi and headed for the main railway station.

The cabby told his passengers, the taxi in which they rode was the last available one in the city. All other vehicles, including those owned by private individuals, were being commandeered by the military.

When they arrived at the main station, one of the Biehl brothers stayed with the cab while Erma hurried into the depot and checked her trunk to the Dutch border. As Biehl had counseled, she bought a second class ticket to London.

From the station, the group went back to the British Consulate. There was still no one to be found.

It was 7:40 a.m. when the taxi took them to the police station. The officers on morning duty had been told of Erma's visit the night before and they had the necessary stamp ready for her passport. With only a few minutes before the 8:04 a.m. train's departure, Biehl ordered the cab driver to stop in front of his home so his family could say goodbye to Erma.

From the taxi, Biehl whistled the first four notes of the hymn, "Do What Is Right", a signal among members of the West German Mission.[2]

Immediately, the windows on the second floor opened and all the Biehls appeared. Sister Biehl was weeping. She called to her husband, telling him that while he was helping Erma that morning, his military summons had arrived. He was to report to his military unit that day. Biehl slumped back in his seat. The taxi raced to the station.

Since, by law, no one could take more than ten marks (about $2.50) out of the country, Erma gave her extra money to Biehl and tearfully said goodbye to her friends. She found a seat on the train and from a window looked for the last time into the faces of Lydia Heibel and President Biehl. All three wept as the train pulled out of the station.[3]

The train rolled toward the city of Emmerich on the German side of the German-Dutch border. In the open fields, manned anti-aircraft guns stood in position.

The Emmerich railway depot, noisy and jammed with hundreds of people attempting to leave Germany, was in a state of wild confusion. Frantic Holland-bound passengers sought in vain for someone who would change their extra marks into Dutch guilders. The money changers, who normally did a brisk and lucrative business in the border station, were nowhere to be found.

The baggage master worked at a furious pace. Almost as quickly as the train came to a halt, the handlers pitched the trunks out of the baggage cars onto the platform. Erma cornered her trunk just as quickly and paid to have it sent on to Holland. She expected to meet other evacuating missionaries in the Emmerich station and was surprised to find she was the only Mormon missionary in the depot.

As her train sped toward Holland, there was little to mark the Dutch Border—only a barbed wire barricade and a line of small concrete blocks intended to obstruct armored tanks.

With a leaden heart, Erma stared out the window. She had spent ten months in Germany, learned the language fairly well and had her genealogy traced. She met and visited with her German relatives and made many friends among the German people. With deep regret and in spite of a war everyone knew would come, she wished she did not have to leave.

At Zevenaar, a small Dutch town not far from the border, the official checked Erma's papers. Her passport was in order and she had a ticket to London. Without opening her baggage, they waved her through.

Again, she was puzzled to find neither missionaries nor Americans in the Zevenaar station.

Erma arrived in Rotterdam sometime during the afternoon. She watched for other missionaries, but, as in all the other stations, there were none. With no idea where the Dutch Mission Office or American Consulate was and with no money to make a phone call, she approached a woman who wore an interpreter's arm band. Had she seen any Americans, any missionaries? The woman shook her head and gestured that she did not understand.

Tired, hungry and feeling totally alone, Erma stood in the rapidly emptying railway station and silently prayed for help.

Then she walked over to the platform gate and peered through the bars. On the other side waited a tall young man, his back to her.

"Do you speak English?" she called.

Startled, the young man jumped and spun around. "Are you one of those?"

"Yes!" she replied with a heart full of relief.

The young man was a Dutch missionary sent to the railway station to watch for the evacuating West German missionaries. Having express orders to remain as inconspicuous as possible, he had been watching for Elders, not a lone Sister.

Erma Rosenhan was the first West German missionary to cross the border into Holland.[4]

Burt Horsley and Richard Poll

From Bremen to the German-Dutch Border was a two-hour ride. The trains were crammed full of people who, like the missionaries, were trying to leave Germany. Burt Horsley and Richard Poll had to stand all the way there.

At the German border, the law required the missionaries to give up any money beyond ten marks. The officials confiscated seventy marks from Poll before allowing the pair to cross the border into Holland.

In Oldenzaal, on the Holland side of the German-Dutch border, the pair received a jolt. Refugees who did not have "through tickets" to London could not enter the country.

The two men tried to explain. They were American missionaries living in Germany. Their mission president had instructed them to go to Rotterdam.

If they wanted to go to Rotterdam, the officials insisted, they must have "through tickets" or the money with which to buy them.

The pair protested that everything was confiscated at the German border. They had no money beyond the ten marks they had been allowed.

"No money?" an officer asked. "How do you expect to live with no money?" He called the station police who arrested the missionaries for vagrancy. While their trunks and luggage sped on to Rotterdam, the missionaries were put under detention in the station.

At length, Horsley and Poll received permission to telephone the Dutch Mission Office. President Franklin J. Murdock advised them to return to Germany on the next train.

When an eastbound train pulled into the Oldenzaal depot, the Dutch officials escorted the missionaries onto it. Within minutes they were headed back to Germany.

In Bentheim, the German border town, the customs agents thoroughly searched their hand luggage. Then an official, using an arrogant tone, ordered the pair to return to Bremen.

Horsley, who was not normally an aggressive young man, angrily reproached the officer for his impertinent attitude. The officer backed down.

Non-residents were not allowed to stay in a border area during a military crisis, he explained. Although they need not go inland as far as Bremen, they must retreat as far as the nearby city of Rheine.

The missionaries arrived in Rheine during the early morning hours of August 26. They went to the post office and asked to put a phone call through to the mission headquarters in Frankfurt. The agent told them that all the lines were being used for priority calls. But if they were willing to wait for a few hours, he would let them know when a line was available. They could try to put the call through then. They agreed to wait.

It was two hours before a line was clear. Horsley talked to President Wood and told him the Dutch border agents would not allow them to enter Holland, that they had no money and were at a loss about what they should do.

President Wood told Horsley to have faith and that he would telegraph eighty marks to them in Rheine. When they received the money, he instructed, they should buy tickets for passage to Copenhagen, Denmark. He also told Horsley to watch for other missionaries who might find themselves in similar circumstances.[5]

In the Frankfurt Mission Office

Five minutes after making arrangements for the money to be wired, the telegraph office called President Wood and told him the telegraph office would no longer accept orders to wire money. "However," she said, "I think I can get your last order through."

Within minutes of that alarming information, the radio announced that beginning Sunday, August 27, at 10:00 p.m. "the

Mission Office Staff hauling luggage to Frankfut train station.

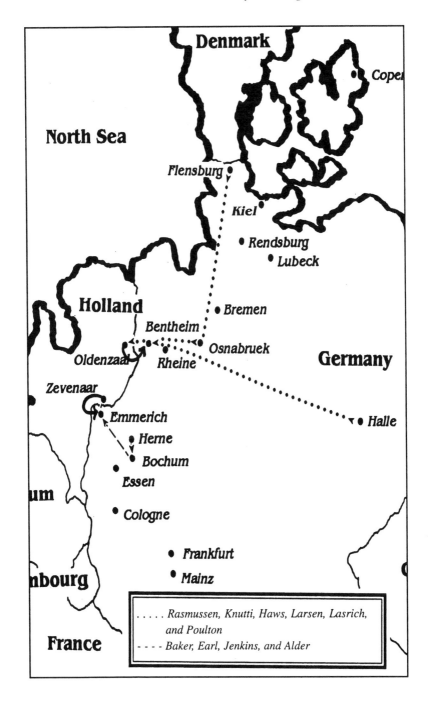

German government will not guarantee anyone his destination on the German railways."

President Wood heard the announcement in stunned silence. At that moment many West German missionaries were on their way to the Dutch border unaware that it was closed to them. Most would be carrying no more than a paltry ten marks, barely enough for a meal. Certainly not enough to get them into Holland or buy a railway ticket to Denmark. They would probably not be able to make connections with the mission office by telephone nor would the office be able to wire money and instructions if they did. And the final blow—within forty-eight hours there would be no scheduled railway services for civilians.[6, 7]

Horsley and Poll

Sore from their one-hundred and fifty mile bicycle trip and having eaten nothing since the day before, Burt Horsley and Richard Poll were tired and hungry. While they waited in the Rheine depot for the money President Wood promised to wire them, they assessed what little they had left and decided to spend it on something to eat.

As they walked through the depot to the restaurant, they noticed a young Jewish woman arguing with the railway officials. The woman recognized the missionaries as Americans and followed them into the restaurant.

She was eighteen years old and the daughter of a Swiss banker. She had been going to school in Germany but her parents, concerned with the increasing Jewish persecutions and the rumors of war, asked her to come home. The young woman carried a large amount of money, a valid Swiss passport and official papers that should have allowed her to leave Germany without a problem. However, the railway agents refused to even sell her a ticket. If the missionaries would help her, she offered, she could well afford to help them.

They agreed to do what they could. She told them she had an idea that could not fail. The station agents would not deny her passage if she was married to an American citizen. If one of them would marry her...

Taken aback, Horsley and Poll refused.

She argued that she was willing to pay them well. With her money they could get out of the country, too.

The pair still refused to consider her suggestion.

The girl offered another plan. With her money they could buy a car and the three of them could run through the border checks.

The missionaries explained in emphatic terms they could not and would not break any governments' laws. They would have no part in such a dangerous scheme.

She begged and pleaded. She offered money and suggested several other reckless ideas which the pair steadfastly rejected.

At last, she settled for the missionaries' offer to go to the depot ticket office and buy tickets for her. They saw her aboard a train bound for Belgium.[8]

Norman Seibold, Adalbert and Elizabeth Goltz

It was not yet light when Norman Seibold left his apartment in Stuttgart. He intended to appoint a man named Ruff as branch president, but the military had other plans for Brother Ruff. He received his military summons only a half hour before Seibold arrived at his home.

Fortunately, a Brother Lutz, whom Seibold deemed worthy, was able to accept responsibility for the branch. Seibold appointed him branch president and turned over the Church records to him.

Then, as President Wood had instructed, Seibold went to Esslingen and the home of Adalbert and Elizabeth Goltz.

The Goltzes were German converts to the Church who immigrated to the United States and raised their family in Utah. After their youngest daughter married, they realized their lifelong dream of returning to their homeland on a mission. The Goltzes proved to be not only hardworking missionaries but effective ones as well.

Seibold informed the pair of President Wood's instructions and advised them to pack as quickly as possible.[9]

Goltz, a former officer in the German cavalry, replied. "It is not necessary for my wife and me to leave. Surely we face no danger in our own Fatherland."[10]

"Whether there is danger or not," Seibold insisted, "President Wood says the missionaries must leave."

Goltz replied, "My patriarchal blessing promised me I would serve a mission in Germany. That promise is not yet fulfilled. I will not go."

Seibold argued but the older man remained unyielding. He would not leave and ordered Seibold from his home.

Seibold refused to be sent away. He turned to Sister Goltz, a shy, modest woman, and said, "Sister Goltz, can't you convince your husband to leave?"

Timidly, Sister Goltz declined to discuss the matter, but she made it plain she would respect her husband's wishes.

Seibold gave up. He returned to the post office and phoned mission headquarters. "They won't come," he told President Wood.

"Yes, they will," he replied. "Go back and get them!"

Seibold returned to the Goltz's apartment. Again he did his best to convince them it was important they leave. And leave now.

Goltz, countered all of Seibold's arguments with "I have faith in my patriarchal blessing. You have not!"

"This is not a matter of faith," Seibold answered heatedly. "This is a matter of obedience. President Wood says we must leave."

In anger, Goltz left the room.

Seibold appealed to Sister Goltz. "Sister Goltz, you've got to do something. President Wood says you've got to leave. The American Consul says you've got to leave. If you don't there's a real good possibility you might be stuck here. If that happens, you'll never see your family again."

About that time Goltz came out of his room and Sister Goltz turned to him and said, "Papa, I go."

"She might just as well have slapped him," Seibold recorded in his journal.

Sister Goltz got her belongings together and when her husband saw she was serious about leaving, he, too, packed his things.[11]

In the Mission Office in Frankfurt

During that Saturday, the mission office began receiving calls from missionaries stranded on the Dutch border.

President Wood telephoned the Dutch Consulate and asked for an explanation of the situation. The Consul expressed surprise. He had no knowledge, until that moment, that the border had been closed.

President Wood also telephoned and spoke to President Franklin J. Murdock of the Dutch Mission. Murdock told him that Erma Rosenhan had crossed the border with no difficulty. "Probably," he said, "because she had a through ticket to London."

With the information that the Dutch border was closed to anyone not having money or "through tickets" and the knowledge they would not be able to use the railway services after 10:00 p.m. the next day, there remained much for the mission office staff to do before they could leave.

First, it was decided, upon the advice of Joseph Fielding Smith, that the temporary mission headquarters should be moved from Holland to Copenhagen, Denmark. That necessitated a second telegram being sent to the missionaries who had not yet left their assigned areas.[12]

Adjustment also had to be made for the office staff; tickets and reservations must be changed and baggage moved.

Because there was no available transportation due to gas rations, the staff had to find a way to move their luggage from the mission home to the railway station.

Several missionaries walked the three-quarters of a mile to the railway station, borrowed a baggage cart and pulled it to the mission office. Then they loaded their luggage on the cart and wrestled it back through the city to the depot.[13]

The last scheduled train was due to leave Frankfurt that evening. Before they left, however, the most important problem was yet to be solved. That of the missionaries stranded at various Dutch border crossings.

Missionaries evacuating from the southern and eastern parts of the mission had been coming into the mission home all during the day. President Wood called several of those to a meeting where he explained that Holland had closed its doors leaving many missionaries stranded and penniless on the border. There was no possibility of wiring instructions and additional money to them. Worst of all, after 10:00 p.m. on Sunday, August 27, the military would take over the railway services and civilians would not be guaranteed they could reach their destinations. Wood proposed that one of the Elders travel to the border towns with the money needed to get the missionaries to either Rotterdam or Copenhagen. He asked for volunteers.

Several missionaries, including Norman Seibold who had just arrived from Stuttgart, raised their hands. President Wood

Earl and Jenkins with new bicycles

dismissed the meeting and then as the men left the room, he asked Seibold to remain.

"Brother, have you ever carried a message to Garcia?"[14]

"No, but I'd be willing to try," he replied.

Seibold was given an envelope containing five hundred marks and tickets to London as well as Copenhagen. He was instructed to travel the railway lines along the Dutch border and search for stranded missionaries. How he found them would be up to him. But his first concern must be that as many as possible were evacuated to a safe country.

It was dark by the time Seibold boarded a train bound for Emmerich on the German border.[15]

Baker, Earl, Alder and Jenkins

Missionaries Grant Baker, Ken Earl, Charles Jenkins Jr. and Alfred Alder spent that entire Saturday morning trying to find a way to get their luggage to the Bochum railway station.

Because of gasoline rationing, the trucks that usually hired out for that type of work were either unavailable or were asking outrageous sums. Baker went into the city in search of a private individual who would lend or rent them a truck.

While Baker was gone, Alder, Jenkins and Earl went into town to sell their bicycles. Though those owned by Jenkins and Earl were very new, they were forced to sell them at a great loss. Thirty marks each, about $7.50.

Alder and Jenkins returned to their Bochum apartment while Earl went to his Herne apartment to finish packing and wait for Baker's return.

After a lengthy wait, Earl decided to move their luggage himself. He managed to move the five large suitcases down the apartment stairs, out to the street and to a street car bound for downtown Bochum.

Upon reaching Bochum, a little more than six miles away, the street car stop was still a considerable distance from the railway station. Again, Earl carried two of the heavy suitcases down the street a short way, left them where he could keep them in sight and went back for the other three. He lugged those beyond the point where he had left the first two. Then he went back for those. By leapfrogging the suitcases, Earl was, at length, able to get all five into the depot.

He checked the luggage on a train bound for Holland, then hurried over to Alder and Jenkins' apartment and helped them move their luggage to the Bochum station.

In the meantime, Baker returned with a truck rented for the outrageous sum of forty marks, (about $10.00) only to find Earl had already moved their luggage.[16]

It was nearly 5:00 p.m. when the four missionaries fought their way to the end of an overcrowded passenger car where they were obliged to sit on their hand luggage.

They arrived in Emmerich two hours later and passed the German border check without difficulty. Within an hour, their train pulled into the railway depot at Zevenaar, Holland.

The Dutch official shepherded the train's passengers through the station and into a large room which was already crowded with Jews trying to leave Germany.

The officers questioned everyone: "Who are you? Where are you going? How much money do you have?"

The four missionaries answered they only had the money they were allowed to take from Germany.

"If you have no money, do you have 'through tickets' to London?" the officer asked.

The missionaries knew nothing of 'through tickets'. They were going to Rotterdam, not London.

Without money or such tickets, the official informed them, they would not be allowed to enter Holland.

Baker and Alder argued that they had been evacuated to Holland the year before during the Czechoslovakian crisis. There had been no difficulties then. Surely some kind of provision could be made. There must be a mistake.

"There is no mistake," the agent told them. He would make no exceptions.

They argued. They cajoled. They plead. But the official remained adamant.

At last, realizing the futility of arguing further, Baker asked for permission to telephone the Dutch Mission Office.

President Murdock told Baker they were to wait in the station and he would send a Dutch missionary with the money they needed to get into Holland. Murdock then spoke to a waitress in the depot restaurant and asked her to feed the stranded missionaries. He promised to send enough money with the Dutch missionary to cover their meals.

The four ate well, but before the Dutch missionary could arrive, an eastbound train pulled into the station. Armed guards rounded up the four missionaries, despite their protests, and the hundreds of Jews in the depot. The guards escorted all of them out of the Zevenaar station and toward a train destined for Emmerich, Germany.

The Jews were hysterical. They argued loudly. Many wept. But the guards refused to allow them to leave the train. One Jewish man, his wife and children looking on in despair, got down on his hands and knees and, clasping a Dutch guard's feet, wept and pleaded that the guard take pity on his family. But it was no use.

Late that night, the missionaries found themselves, once more, in the Emmerich railway station. Baker recorded in his journal that the customs agents thoroughly searched the missionaries' luggage "as if we were coming into the country for the first time and going to bomb the place."

In the meantime, using a silver dollar Jenkins had hidden from the officials, Baker telephoned Frankfurt.

President Wood told Baker that Norman Seibold was on his way to the border with money and "through tickets" to London. He instructed them to wait in Emmerich until Seibold arrived. Then they could proceed to Rotterdam.

Denmark

Copen

North Sea

Flensburg

Kiel

Hamburg

Rendsburg

Lubeck

Holland

Bremen

Bentheim

Oldenzaal

Rheine

Osnabruek

Germany

Zevenaar

Emmerich

Halle

Herne

Bochum

Essen

Cologne

um

Frankfurt

bourg

Mainz

- - - - *Bingham, Loertscher, Dean, Mabey, Meyer, and Woolf*
. . . . . *Marrott and the Rieglers*

About midnight, the missionaries laid down on the wooden benches in the second class waiting room and tried to get some rest.[17]

Vern Marrott and the Rieglers

Vern Marrott rose at 7:00 a.m. after only an hour and a half of sleep. Although most of the packing for the Rieglers and himself had been completed the night before, he still had to pick up their laundry, which was done every week by a Sister Berg.

That morning, columns of soldiers and military vehicles filled the Mainz streets. Marrott found it necessary to dodge and weave through the long lines of traffic to reach the street car stop. He found Albert Berg's fiancee waiting there.

"When she saw me there with my suitcase, she looked as if a charge of electricity had gone through her," Marrott wrote in his journal.

The two spoke for a moment. She, like many other Latter-day Saints in Germany, believed while the missionaries were there, everything would be all right. There would be no war.

She and Albert had been engaged for a year, she told Marrott. They had planned and saved for the time they could be married. But now...The girl's eyes filled with tears and despair and she turned away, unable to speak.

The Berg's hoped Marrott would not come that morning but they expected him just the same. With the German army mobilizing on the Polish border, the Prophet would know it was too dangerous to allow the missionaries to stay in Germany.

Sister Berg wept as she folded his laundry and put it in the suitcase. Then Marrott said a tearful goodbye to the family and left.

Back at his apartment, Marrott was unable to finish his breakfast before the station agent arrived to pick up their trunks. Then he and the Rieglers walked with the agent to the depot.

It seemed that everywhere—in the streets, in the shops, and in the railway station—there were soldiers. Their jackboots shining, the officers swaggered with self-importance. The new recruits, dressed in heavy woollen uniforms and boots, looked uncomfortable that hot sultry, summer day. Many soldiers were drunk and fist fights broke out in the station.

The depot was also crowded with foreigners and Jews, all trying to get out of Germany before the 10:00 deadline tomorrow night.

The train, a half hour late, was already overloaded but Marrott managed to get Sister Riegler into a car. But the conductor refused to allow Brother Riegler aboard.

"There are too many people already!" he shouted above the confusion.

Determined, Marrott pushed and shoved until he cleared a small space for Brother Riegler and helped him board the train.

The train was so crowded no one could sit down. The three missionaries stood during the one hundred-mile ride to Cologne. The Rieglers were not strong and the long uncomfortable ride on that sweltery day was physically taxing for them.

In the Cologne station, the passengers thinned out, leaving only foreigners and Jews aboard the train. To Marrott's relief, the Rieglers were at last able to sit down.

Just across the Dutch border, in Zevenaar, the officials questioned the passengers. The missionaries, as well as several Jews and a Czechoslovakian, were taken aside and asked to wait in a small room in the depot.

In alarm, Marrott watched from a window as their train, with their trunks aboard, pulled out of the station bound for Rotterdam. It disappeared down the tracks.

Then a Dutch officer appeared and instructed the group to follow him. He took them to a platform where guards herded them into a dilapidated passenger train. Within minutes they were headed back to the German border.

Marrott and the Rieglers got off the train in Emmerich. Not knowing what else to do, they waited in the depot until a station agent informed them they must leave the border area.

The three discussed their dilemma. There was nothing to do but move farther inland. In a larger city they might have a better chance of meeting other evacuating missionaries and get help.

It was after 1:00 a.m. when their train pulled into the Cologne depot. They tried to telephone the Frankfurt Mission Office but all the lines were being used for priority calls.

With no money and no other alternative, the three waited in the station on one of the many platforms. They had had little sleep the night before and nothing to eat for nearly twenty-four hours. The Rieglers were totally exhausted.

They found some vacant benches and laid down.[18]

Rasmussen and Knutti

Ellis Rasmussen and Frank Knutti walked through the streets of Halle. Although it was early morning, the crowds had already gathered outside the newspaper office, waiting for the latest news.

"Eastward, the armies are racing, pushing, blasting their way to free the oppressed Germans in the Corridor," the papers declared. "Hitler can do anything and everything!"[19]

The bold headlines did not inspire great enthusiasm among the people on the street, however. Many walked away muttering and shaking their heads.

The missionaries continued down the street until they found a shop where they spent their extra marks on photography equipment. Then they boarded a train for the Dutch border.

At the German border town, Bentheim, they met Louis J. Haws and Claytor Larsen from Nordhausen. The four crossed the border together, arriving at Oldenzaal, Holland.

In the Dutch station, a customs agent collected their passports and directed them to wait in a small room. As they waited, Ben Lasrich and Donald Poulton from Flensburg arrived and joined them.

After a long wait, the agent returned and informed them, in no uncertain terms, that since they had no money and no "through tickets", they would not be allowed to enter Holland.

In surprise and dismay the missionaries argued they did not intend to remain in Holland but while they were there the Church would take full responsibility for them. Surely, someone had explained that to them.

The missionaries were no exception to the law and the official had no time to listen to their arguments. An armed guard escorted the group to a small, motor-driven train, returned their passports and sent them back to Germany.

In Bentheim, Lasrich attempted to telephone President Murdock in Holland. After many frustrating technical delays, the operator connected him to the Dutch Mission Office.

President Murdock assured Lasrich that he would see what could be done for them. He told him he would call back with further information.

Feeling relieved, the missionaries relaxed in the station's waiting room. It was not long, however, before a border policeman ordered them out of the depot and threatened them with arrest if they continued to loiter in the station.

The young men pooled what little money they had, left a message to forward their expected telephone call and rented a room in the nearby Kaiserhoff hotel.[20]

Bingham and Loertscher

In Lubeck, John Bingham and Joseph Loertscher were up after a restful night's sleep, recovered from their unfortunate bicycle trip in the Schleswig Holstein with seven other missionaries.

As they prepared for their morning devotional, the 8:00 a.m. mail arrived. In it, were two letters from the American Consul advising the Americans to leave Germany.

They barely had time to read the letters when their landlady, Frau Wilbourney, appeared at their door. With tears in her eyes, she handed them a special delivery telegram.

"Leave immediately for Rotterdam..."

After they finished packing, they called and set apart Herman Meyer, a Priest, to be the branch president.

When Loertscher arrived in Flensburg only a few weeks before, he had been required to temporarily surrender his passport to the local police. By that Saturday morning, however, they had not yet returned it to him. Since he could not leave the country without it, the two realized they must retrieve it themselves.

Their bicycle trip to the Kiel conference and trip to the Schleswig Holstein had taken only three days but in those three days the once-peaceful city of Lubeck had become a scene of dramatic activity. Long lines of fully-equipped soldiers marched through the city while military trucks rumbled over the cobblestone streets. Crews unloaded and stacked sandbags in front of public buildings. Plate glass windows were boarded up. Blackout curtains hung in windows and doorways.

The gasoline stations were closed. Taxi cabs and all privately owned vehicles had been commandeered by the army. The city

John Bingham in Lubeck railway station 26 August 1939.
Note the German Soldiers' equipment in lower left hand corner.

buses still ran but they were loaded to capacity. Everywhere, people hurried through the streets.

A constable at the police station told the pair that Loertscher's passport had been sent to a military office.

At the military office, an official placed the young men under arrest because Loertscher was not carrying a passport.

The missionaries explained they had been sent there by a police constable. They also explained the police constable had told them Loertscher's passport was in that military office.

"It is not here," the official insisted.

The pair was released and told they would have to return to the police station.

The police officer referred them to another military office.

That morning, the missionaries went from the police station to various military offices four times before Loertscher's passport was located in the desk of the first police constable they had spoken to.

The morning was gone when they raced back to their rooms. Their train left at 1:00 p.m. and they still had a lot to do. In vain, they attempted to find someone to move their trunks to the railway station. What luggage they could not carry would have to be left behind.

There was also the problem of money. Bingham's parents had recently sent him three hundred dollars so that when he was released in a few weeks he could tour Europe before going home. It would have been simple enough for Bingham to spend the money on souvenirs, as many missionaries had done. However, he could not bring himself to do that. Instead, both missionaries decided to leave their extra marks with Frau Wilbourney.

After saying goodbye, Bingham and Loertscher rushed to the station, arriving ten minutes too late for the one o'clock train. They checked the schedules. Another train, the last connection to Holland, was leaving the station at 3:00 p.m. They sat down and waited.

The hot, humid depot was crowded beyond description. "I've never seen anything like it," Loertscher wrote.

There were soldiers, some headed toward Poland, others going home on leave, foreigners trying to get out of the country before Sunday's deadline. And countless Jews, desperate to be anywhere but in Germany.

The train, a "snellzug" (fast train) with double-decker cars, pulled into the station filled beyond capacity. The crowds on the platform surged forward, pushing ad shoving as they tried to board the train. Some, in desperation, climbed through the windows. The two young men at last managed to squeeze into one of the cars.

Spending several long hours in that miserably confined condition, the pair arrived at the Hamburg railway depot where they were to change trains. After more pushing and shoving, they struggled out of the crowded car.

As they walked through the station, the familiar strains of "Come, Come Ye Saints" sung in English, floated on the air. They followed the sound to a railroad passenger car on a nearby track.[21]

There, among the occupants of yet another crowded compartment, sat John Dean and Edward Mabey from Kiel. Bingham and Loertscher passed their hand luggage through the open window to Dean and Mabey and then squeezed into the compartment.

After a seven-hour ride, they emerged from the train in Oldenzaal, Holland, cramped, overheated and exhausted. They found Lawrence J. Meyer and Wilford Woolf already in the Dutch station.

The border officials took the missionaries' passports and asked them to wait. After what seemed like hours, the officers returned their papers and directed them to another train. They soon discovered, to their great dismay, they were not traveling west to Rotterdam, but east back into Germany.[22]

ENDNOTES

1 Leland Blatter's Missionary Journal.

2 According to an explanation written by Erma Rosenhan, "Do What Is Right" was the favorite hymn of a German Saint, Paul Kuepper. It was he who began whistling the first four notes of the song to draw the attention of other members. This method was used first in Kuepper's hometown of Essen and quickly spread throughout the mission.

3 According to Henry Haurand of Bountiful, Utah, President Walter Biehl was killed in combat. Haurand is Walter Biehl's nephew.

4 Rosenhan account.

5 Reconstructed from conversations with A. Burt Horsley and Richard D. Poll.

6 President Wood's account of the evacuation, "The Lord Stood at Our Side," was taken from a conference speech he delivered on Saturday, 6 April 1940. The address was printed in the Deseret News Church Section of 15 June 1940. In that speech, he stated the railway deadline was Sunday, August 27, at midnight. Of the other accounts written by former West German missionaries, the majority agree the deadline was actually 10:00 p.m.

7 Wood address.

8 Horsley and Poll interviews.

9 Norman Seibold interview.

10 Lucille Goltz Stringham, daughter of Elizabeth and Adalbert Goltz.

11 Seibold interview.

12 Wood address.

13 Elmer Tueller account.

14 Between 1895 and 1898, Calixto Garcia led Cuba in revolt against Spain. During the war, Army Lieutenant Andrew S. Rowan, sought out Garcia in the jungles of Cuba with an offer of aid from the United States.

The incident inspired an essay by Elbert Hubbard entitled "A Message to Garcia". Later, the essay was developed into a movie script of the same name with stars Barbara Stanwyck, John Payne and Wallace Beery.

15 Seibold interview and Wood address.

16 Owen Ken Earl account.

17 Reconstructed from a personal interview with Grant Baker, written accounts from Charles Jenkins Jr. and Own Ken Earl.

18 Vern Marrott tape.

19 Rasmussen, Ellis T., "Border Incident, Inside Germany," *The Improvement Era* (Dec. 1943, pp. 752-3, 793).

20 Reconstructed from the Rasmussen article, a personal interview with Frank Knutti, a written account from Louis J. Haws and the mission journal of Ben Lasrich.

21 Brigadier General John W. Dean account and the Loertscher account.

22 Dean account, Loertscher account and Lawrence J. Meyer account.

—THREE—

SUNDAY, 27 AUGUST 1939

On the Way to Denmark

Horsley, Poll, Bingham, Loertscher, Dean, Mabey, Meyer and Woolf.

It was midnight in the city of Rheine. Having just received the eighty marks President Wood wired, Burt Horsley and Richard Poll waited in the railway station for their train.

As it pulled in and stopped, the two were surprised to hear the whistled notes of "Do What is Right". From one of the cars emerged John Dean, Edward Mabey, Lawrence Meyer, Wilford Woolf, John Bingham and Joseph Loertscher. They had just been turned back at the Dutch border.[1]

The eight missionaries pooled their money and found they had enough for tickets as far as Hamburg. Even at that late hour, the trains were greatly overcrowded and the young men felt lucky to have room to stand. It was another five hours to Hamburg and, exhausted as they were, they worried about what they would do once they got there.

Bingham lamented that his three hundred dollars, left with Frau Wilbourney in Lubeck, was several hours beyond Hamburg. How they all wished it was in his pocket.

The missionaries decided they would try to get Bingham to Lubeck so he could retrieve his money. It would be more than enough to ensure all of them passage to Copenhagen.

At Osnabruck, Wesley Knudsen and Ralph Thompson climbed into the other missionaries' car. Between them, the two had a little money. It was just enough to lend to John Dean.

Before Dean left Kiel, he had taken the time to go to the bank and close his account. He asked that the money be wired to the United States. Before it could be sent to America, however, it would have to be processed through a bank in Hamburg. If the money had already left Kiel and if he could intercept it in the Hamburg bank before it was sent on to the U.S., some of their money problems would be over.

The train pulled into the Hamburg station and Dean, using Knudsen and Thompson's money, hired a cab and raced across the city to the bank. The officials were just putting his money on the wire as he arrived.

Dean's money was not much, but it was enough to buy the ten missionaries passage to Lubeck where Bingham could get his money from Frau Wilbourney.[2]

Richard Poll wrote in his journal:

> My impression of the trip and the ride into Lubeck was a train bulging with soldiers, young fellows, not at all belligerent looking, with trench equipment, guns and tin hats. Somehow, those German helmets always looked more formidable, more businesslike than any worn by any other soldiers. The other fellows were just as sleepy looking as we were.
>
> I couldn't help thinking that if their environment had been different, they'd have been about like us instead of cogs in a war machine and possibly dead in a few hours or days.
>
> Those guys, much smaller than I, were lugging packs that would bow my legs. Nazism had built some fine physical specimens, but "Why?"
>
> I guess I was in a pretty poor frame of mind.

At Lubeck, while the others had something to eat, John Bingham sent a message to his landlady, Frau Wilbourney. At length, she appeared with the money Bingham and Loertscher had left with her. She also brought their trunks.

The missionaries took just enough money for tickets to Copenhagen, remembering they could take no more than ten marks out of the country.

At the German-Danish border town of Warnemunde, two more missionaries, Harold E. Kratzer and Richard Larkin Glade, joined the other ten. The twelve missionaries made a somber group as they passed through customs.

Poll wrote:

> Tired from pessimistic and morbid reflections about human folly. All the other Elders were in bad moods, too. Even the arrival of Elders Kratzer and Glade, two usually jovial eggs, didn't put much life in the party.

The customs officials challenged the missionaries, saying such strong, healthy young men would serve the Fuhrer well. They could go far in the military service and, after the war was over, they would be made "obermeisters" in the conquered American provinces.

In dour moods, the missionaries ignored the challenge.

Their train, minus the engine, was loaded on to a ferry and shipped across the Baltic Sea to Denmark.

That evening at 6:00 p.m., ten travel-weary and discouraged missionaries arrived in safe, sane Copenhagen.[3]

The Smiths Go To Denmark

Since most of the missionaries, including those of the East German Mission, had been re-routed from Holland to Denmark, Apostle Joseph Fielding Smith knew he needed to be in Copenhagen as quickly as possible.

In his hotel room in Holland that morning of Sunday, August 27, Smith asked for airline reservations to Copenhagen. The airline agent told him there were no available tickets. Reservations had to be made days in advance.

Smith asked the agent to telephone him when two tickets became available.

The agent was not encouraging. He repeated, "There are no reservations and no tickets available." And he would not guarantee he could provide the tickets any time soon.

Again, Smith asked him to call when the reservations were available.

A few hours later, Smith's telephone rang. It was the ticket agent. Someone had canceled their reservations at the last minute. There were two vacant seats on the next flight to Denmark.

By that evening, Apostle Joseph Fielding and Jesse Evans Smith were in Copenhagen.[4]

The Mission Office Staff in Frankfurt

It was dark when the West German Mission Office staff, including President and Sister Wood and their two young daughters, walked through Frankfurt to the railway station. Their train was due to depart at midnight but was an hour late.

At Kassel, their train was commandeered for troop transport and the group was forced to wait on the station platform until another north-bound train arrived.

They were again "bumped off" at Hanover and at Hamburg. Each time the group waited in the station until they could board another train headed north. Frequently, their train was pulled off onto side tracks while troop trains passed.

From Hamburg, they went to Lubeck, from Lubeck to Rostock which was only a few miles from Warnemunde. Warnemunde was the town where their train was to board the ferry for Denmark. But at Rostock, the engineer and fireman stopped the engine and left the train. The missionaries were told the train would go no farther.

According to J. Richard Barnes, the missionaries took matters into their own hands. When the crew had disconnected the cars from the engine and left the station, the mission office staff and the missionaries traveling with them got in the engine. Someone figured out how to use the controls and put the train into motion, heading for the dock at Warnemunde.

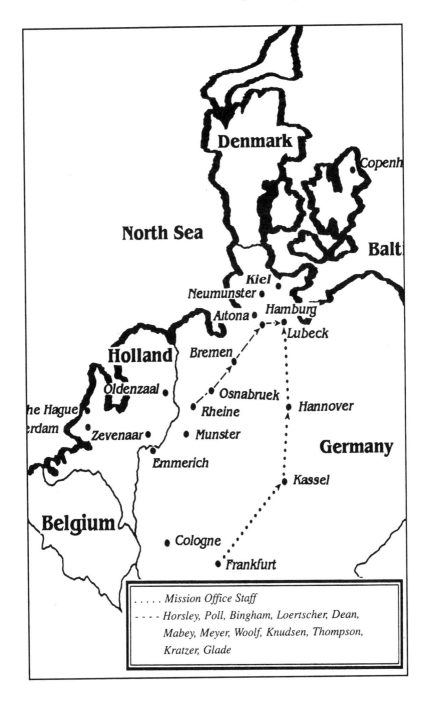

..... Mission Office Staff
- - - - Horsley, Poll, Bingham, Loertscher, Dean,
         Mabey, Meyer, Woolf, Knudsen, Thompson,
         Kratzer, Glade

As they approached the dock, the ferry was just beginning to pull away. The missionaries leaned out the windows and shouted, calling for the ferry captain to wait for them. Several missionaries, who had small American flags in their luggage, waved them. The ferry captain redocked and members of the crew rushed to help them aboard.

They left the pilfered engine at Warnemunde and crossed the Baltic Sea to Denmark. It was late that night when they were greeted by President Mark Garff of the Danish Mission.[5]

Rasmussen, Knutti, Lasrich, Poulton, Haws and Larsen

Although still weary in body and mind, Ben Lasrich could sleep no longer and got up early that Sunday morning. Worried at having received no further word from President Murdock, he left the Kaiserhoff Hotel where he and five others had spent the night. He went to the post office and asked if there had been any telephone calls for them.

The official shook his head. "No calls."

In an effort to save what little money they had left, the missionaries decided to pretend the morning was a Fast Sunday. But there was no pretending the hunger pains were anything else. About noon they went down town and bought a bag of rolls and a jar of jam. It was a scant meal, but it filled the empty places for a while.

After they had eaten, they checked the post office again. Still no calls.

At the railway station, the attendant told them no one had left a message for them there.

Despondent, some missionaries thought the situation could grow no worse. They were wrong.

About two o'clock the Gestapo caught up with the missionaries. The blackshirted officers ordered them to be out of Bentheim by 4:00 p.m.

Alarmed, Lasrich went to the post office again and succeeded in reaching President Murdock in Rotterdam.

President Murdock told Lasrich they had been trying to reach him for hours but could not make contact. He told Lasrich the missionaries should "sit tight". If they had not heard from the Dutch Mission Office by 4:00 p.m., they were to return to the border and attempt another crossing at Oldenzaal. He also told Lasrich that a Dutch missionary, John Robert Kest, was on his way to the Oldenzaal station to meet them. Kest would be carrying "through tickets" and money.

Lasrich went back to the hotel room and he and the others tried to rest.[6]

John Robert Kest of the Dutch Mission

In the early hours of that Sunday morning, John Robert Kest, a fair-haired Californian, boarded a train in The Hague, Holland. With him, he carried more than three hundred Dutch guilders as well as "through tickets" to London.

Because of increased rail traffic, the two hour trip took four hours. It was after 11:00 a.m. when Kest's train pulled into the Oldenzaal, Holland station. But there was no sign of the missionaries who had telephoned the Dutch Mission Office the night before. Puzzled, Kest approached the station master.

"Yes, some young American missionaries were in the station last night. They did not have 'through tickets' or money and were returned to Bentheim, Germany," he told Kest. "They have not crossed back into Oldenzaal since."

Kest decided to try to telephone a message to the missionaries in Bentheim. After three frustrating hours, Kest abandoned the attempt. He telephoned President Murdock.

"Use your own judgment as to what should be done, Elder Kest."

Kest turned the matter over in his mind. The only thing for him to do, he decided, was to go to Bentheim and find the missionaries himself.

A simple solution, except for one major problem. Kest had no visa to enter Germany. He spent the next hour on the telephone with the American Consulate trying to arrange for a visa. He tried the American Embassy in The Hague. He heard the same story at both offices.

Thousands of desperate people, some attempting to leave Germany, others trying to arrange visas for friends and loved ones, had deluged the offices with telegrams and telephone calls. Their office staffs were working eighteen hour shifts to handle the mountainous volume of paperwork. They were sorry, but they could not help him.

Kest returned to the station master and discussed the situation with him. Kest explained that he had sufficient funds to guarantee the missionaries would not become indigent and he also had "through tickets" to London for them.

The station master shook his head. Overnight the Dutch government had changed its policy again. No one seeking refuge, no matter how much money he had, was being allowed into Holland.

Solemnly, Kest digested that bit of information. Neither the money nor the "through tickets" he carried would be of any use to the German missionaries. They couldn't get into Holland. But, if they had tickets for Denmark, they might make it to Copenhagen. Kest came to a dangerous decision. He would have to buy tickets to Denmark, cross the border and go into Bentheim whether he had a visa or not. He would find the West German missionaries there and give them the tickets.

With the money President Murdock had given him, Kest bought ten tickets to Copenhagen in the Oldenzaal depot. Then he boarded a train bound for Bentheim, Germany. To his immense relief and surprise, the Dutch officials did not ask to see a visa.

As the train sped toward the German border, Kest had grave doubts whether his decision was the correct one. He was traveling without a legal permit into hostile Germany. He hoped the missionaries he was supposed to find were still in Bentheim. And he prayed he would be able to find them.

At last, the train pulled into the Bentheim station and stopped. Kest wrote:

> A moment later there was a sharp clicking of heels. German blackshirts stepped quickly through the car, their eyes cold as steel, taking in at a glance the occupants of each car. Handing the leader my passport, the inevitable question was shot at me:
>
> "Why is no visa stamped on the proper page?"
>
> This thought flashed through my mind: "Elder Kest, you have always enjoyed acting. If you have ever acted a part well, do it now!"
>
> I explained to them in exasperatingly slow and deliberately incoherent English that at present I was living in Holland, had heard that some of my friends were in Bentheim and, knowing that railroad and train transportation was being curtailed, wanted to visit them while still possible to do so.
>
> Suspicion shown from the cold eyes of the officers.
>
> I rambled on, hoping all the while they would have great difficulty understanding me, which they did.
>
> Suddenly, curtly came the question: "Can you speak no Dutch? No German?"
>
> "No," I replied. "I've only been here a comparatively short while and have not learned the languages well. A few simple phrases I can understand. Nothing more."
>
> It was fortunate that the German officer in charge spoke rather poor English. As I went on, talking disjointedly, tossing in a Dutch or German phrase here and there, the effect I wished to produce took hold of the men. They must have concluded that here was a simple, foolish American trying to see some friends for no good reason.
>
> Inside the little cubicle in the station where they had taken me for questioning, they searched me thoroughly.
>
> What would they do to the precious tickets which I had in my suit coat pocket?
>
> They confiscated binder, papers, passport, all the money on my person and started going through each pocket in both my coat

and vest. I took the ten tickets out of my pocket and placed them on the table before me. No one seemed to see the tickets!

The officer in charge gave me a receipt for the money, binder, papers and all my personal effects, and said, "You have forty minutes to catch the return train to Holland. After that time we cannot guarantee your safety."

Taking the tickets from the table, I stuffed them in my pocket. Not an eye flickered. I had the strong impression that the action had been entirely unobserved. Hurriedly, I left the station, my knees weak, my palms sweating!

Kest went out to the street and began asking those he met if they had seen any young Americans. No one had but, at last, someone suggested he check at the Kaiserhoff Hotel.

At 3:30 p.m., only a half hour before the Gestapo deadline, a harried Kest banged on the missionaries' hotel room door.

I quickly told them that these tickets from Holland might, with luck, ensure their passage to Copenhagen. "You must leave immediately, Brethren, and try to make connections into Denmark, as all railroad transportation is being cut off at an alarming rate!"

The Elders needed no urging, and in less than five minutes were ready, having very little luggage with them.

Quickly kneeling down, we held a prayer circle and asked our Father that we might be safely conducted to our respective destinations. As the seven of us knelt in fervent prayer, we all felt a closeness and unity experienced very infrequently in life. We were truly united and prayed with power and faith, believing our requests would be granted, for we realized the desperate nature of our situation.

I hurried back to the office of the Blackshirts where my passport and effects were being held. The station master gave me my papers and money immediately, but a Blackshirt guard stuck my passport in his wide cuff and marched insolently before me as the passengers boarded the train for Holland.

The whistle of the train was blowing and I noticed the clock indicated only three minutes until departure time. Finally, the Blackshirt strutted over and, with a sneer, handed me my passport, muttering some deprecatory remark under his breath. He pushed me to the ticket window where I was obliged to buy a German ticket to Oldenzaal even though my Dutch ticket assured passage to Bentheim and return.

It was necessary to run in order to catch the train—the wheels had just begun to turn. I sank into the seat, grateful for the Brethren's escape and my own now certain and safe return."[7]

Rasmussen, Knutti, Lasrich, Poulton, Haws and Larsen

Although they had been "rescued" by John Kest, the ordeal of the six West German missionaries was not yet over.

Kest's tickets to Copenhagen originated in Oldenzaal, Holland. Having never been in that city, the missionaries worried that a German official would question their possession of the tickets. In that case they would be detained and arrested.

One of them suggested they fold back the ticket book cover, which identified Oldenzaal as the city of departure, and hoped the officials did not inspect the tickets too closely.

Lasrich approached the depot gate and handed his ticket book to the agent, who checked it, stamped it and allowed Lasrich onto the platform. The agent did not bother to check the other men's booklets, but stamped them and waved them through the gate.

Anticipating a change of trains at Salzbergen, they again grew anxious. With the railway service running on a confused and much-interrupted schedule and their own train late, they worried that their connection there would leave without them.

When they arrived at the Salzbergen depot, their train was miraculously waiting on the tracks. The station officials had decided to hold it over for the passengers arriving from Bentheim.

Relieved, the missionaries boarded the train and sped on to Osnabruck.[8]

Norman Seibold's "Message to Garcia"

It was 4:00 a.m. when Norman Seibold's train pulled into the large Cologne railway station. The depot was massed with people. Vacationers trying to get home before the Sunday deadline and Jews and foreigners hoping for any train which would carry them out of Germany.

Seibold, a strapping young man of over two hundred pounds, was an Idaho farm boy who had played football for the University of Utah. He fought his way out of the crowded railway car and looked up and down the platform. There were so many people in the vast Cologne depot, how on earth could he hope to find a few stranded missionaries? But this did not discourage Seibold, who had been given a special mission and who had faith that heavenly help would be provided.

Seibold, who claims he could never whistle, climbed onto a nearby baggage cart and pursed his lips and blew. Out came the first four notes of "Do What Is Right".

A few people turned to stare. Seibold drew another long breath and whistled the tune again. From the crowded platform appeared Ferryle McOmber and President Walter Biehl. Biehl was on his way to join his military unit.

With only minutes before the train was to depart, Seibold briefly explained he had been sent by President Wood to search for stranded missionaries along the Dutch border. The two other men offered to help.

Their combined efforts, as they hurried in different directions through the depot whistling the notes of "Do What Is Right", netted fellow missionaries Dean Griner and William Manning. Those two were also stranded and without funds or tickets.[9]

At the other end of the Cologne railway station, Vern Marrott awakened from a restless sleep. He roused the elderly Rieglers. "Another train has come into the station," he told them. "There has to be help for us somewhere. Maybe it's on this train."

As he walked down into the tunnel between the platforms, Marrott whistled the notes of "Do What Is Right".

He stopped. He wasn't sure he had heard it. The sound came again and nearly stopped his heart. Someone was whistling "Do What Is Right". He hurried up to the platform and there found Norman Seibold.

Seibold handed Marrott an envelope and said, "I'm not going to take the time to explain now because there is none. Just get on this train and then open the envelope. You'll find instructions inside."

Marrott raced back for the Rieglers and when he had settled them in the train, he opened the envelope. In it were tickets to London by way of The Hague, Holland. Marrott sighed with relief. There would be no difficulty now.

It was nearly 9:00 a.m. when the missionaries disembarked at the Emmerich, Germany station. There, they found Grant Baker, Ken Earl, Charles Jenkins Jr. and Alfred Alder.

A train bound for Zevenaar, Holland was leaving within minutes. Because Marrott, Griner, Manning and the Rieglers had already received their "through tickets", they boarded the train. Seibold and McOmber stayed in the Emmerich station to brief Baker, Earl, Alder and Jenkins.

As Marrott helped the ailing Rieglers onto the train, Ken Earl heard Marrott mutter to himself, "Wir muss gehen. Wir muss gehen." (We must get through. We must get through!")

Marrott, The Rieglers, Manning and Griner

In the Dutch station of Zevenaar, the Rieglers, Marrott, Manning and Griner waited in the customs line. Soberly they watched their fellow passengers being turned away. "No refugees," the officials told them sternly.

Marrott glanced at the Rieglers who had slumped onto a nearby bench, their faces ashen with exhaustion.

"We've got to get through," Marrott said repeatedly. "Those old people aren't going to make it if we don't."

When their turn came, Marrott shepherded the older couple through customs. The officials checked their passports, stamped their tickets and waved them back onto the Holland-bound train.

As the three were getting settled, Marrott glanced out the window. Griner and Manning were arguing with the border agents who refused to let them reboard the train. Marrott heard the roar of the train's engine, the whistle blew and the wheels began to turn. Griner and Manning were still on the platform in a heated conversation with the customs agents. It was Marrott's last glimpse of them as the train pulled out of the station.[10, 11]

Norman Seibold in Emmerich

Still in the Emmerich depot, Norman Seibold took out the money President Wood had given him and detailed the plan to McOmber, Baker, Earl, Alder and Jenkins. With that money they could all cross the border into Holland.

Unfortunately, the group attracted the suspicion of an Emmerich City policeman who happened to be on the station platform. The policeman probably saw the large roll of cash Seibold held in his hand and suspected the group of attempting to smuggle money out of Germany.

The policeman walked over to the missionaries and demanded to know what they were doing. He ordered everyone to turn their pockets inside out and open their wallets. Seibold showed him the five hundred marks.

"Give it to me!" the policeman commanded.

"Over my dead body," countered Seibold.

The officer's face darkened. "Very well, but I must insist that you come with me to the police station."

"I don't have to go anywhere with you," retorted Seibold. "You have no authority here. "I'll talk to the military police but I won't leave this station."

Aware of the watching crowd, the policeman drew himself up with great authority and said, "You are coming with me. Now!"

"I won't. I'm an American citizen! I demand to see the military police!"

The officer made a move to take hold of Seibold, who resisted. "Don't you dare touch me. If you do, there's going to be a fight!"

The policeman hesitated, uncertain.

"I'm an American citizen! I demand to see the military police!"

Nervously, the officer glanced around at the astonished crowd. All eyes were on him. It was his move. "All right," he said.

The officer escorted Seibold and Ken Earl to an office in the inner recesses of the depot. Earl had been found in possession of twenty marks instead of the allowable ten.

The military police captain heard the account of the incident with an expressionless face. His eyes were hard and cold. When the policeman finished, the captain, in harsh tones and strong language, reminded the officer that city policemen had no authority in a railway station. He ordered the officer to leave the depot and not return.

The captain turned his attention to the two missionaries who stood before his desk and demanded an explanation.

When Seibold finished, the captain nodded. He knew of the Mormons. He could easily understand why the missionaries must leave Germany.

"I'm going to write a pass for you," the captain told Seibold. "If you have any difficulties in the railway stations as you leave, just show this to the proper authorities." He folded the sheet of paper and handed it to Seibold who tucked it in his coat pocket.

The pair left the captain's office, Earl still in possession of his twenty marks and Seibold with the precious five hundred. They joined the other waiting Elders in the station and the six proceeded to Zevenaar, Holland on the next train.

At the Dutch station, they found Dean Griner and William Manning. "The Dutch officials wouldn't let us cross," they told Seibold.

"Where are Elder Marrott and the Rieglers?" he asked.

Denmark

Copenhage

North Sea

Baltic

Kiel
Neumunster
Altona   Hamburg
Lubeck

Holland

Bremen
Bentheim
Oldenzaal   Osnabruek
Hague   Rheine   Hannover
dam   Zevenaar   Munster
Emmerich

Kassel

Germany

Belgium

——— Seibold, McOmber, Manning, Griner, Baker, Earl
Alder, Jenkins, Lasrich, Poulton, Haws, Larsen,
Rasmussen, Knutti

Griner and Manning shrugged in bewilderment. "The border agents turned us back but Marrott and the Rieglers passed through without a hitch."

In his journal for that date, Seibold wrote:

> That those two old people got through shall be a testimony to me as long as I live. What we went through in the next twenty-four hours, those old people could never have stood.[12]

Denmark?

At the Zevenaar station, the border officials rounded up Seibold, McOmber, Manning, Griner, Baker, Earl, Jenkins and Alder and herded them through the station. As they crossed the railroad tracks toward the waiting trains, they saw a Dutch missionary waving a fist-full of money.

He shouted to them, "I have money from President Murdock for you." But the Dutch official refused to allow the missionaries to stop and talk to him. He also refused to allow him to pass the money to the Germany-bound missionaries.

The German missionaries shrugged, waved goodbye to the Dutch missionary and climbed onto the waiting train. It was the second round-trip for Baker, Earl, Alder and Jenkins.

It was 1:00 p.m. when they arrived at the now familiar Emmerich railway station. They discussed what they would do. The Belgian, French and Swiss borders had already closed, or would be closing in the next few hours. Their only hope of escape from Germany appeared to be through Denmark.[13]

Although the government announced that the regular railway services would continue until 10:00 p.m., the missionaries discovered the train schedules were no longer in effect. The station agents could not tell them when the next train would be arriving and departing nor where it would be going. Neither could they guarantee them their destinations. But the missionaries had to try.[14]

Using part of the money President Wood gave Seibold, they bought any available passage left in the ticket office. The next train into the station was headed north to Hamburg. The missionaries climbed on.

At Munster they were "bumped off". They were told the train was "for military personnel only."

When the next north-bound train pulled in, the missionaries were refused passage. This train, too, was solely for troop transport. Undaunted, the young men decided when the next north-bound train came in they would take matters into their own hands.

After what seemed like hours, another train arrived at the Munster station bulging with soldiers and pulling flat cars loaded with tanks and trucks. One of the missionaries walked up to the engineer and casually asked, "In what direction are you headed?"

"North," the engineer replied.

The missionary signaled the others who waited on the platform. As unobtrusively as possible they gathered their hand luggage. The train whistle blew. Heavy wheels began to turn. The missionaries watched and waited. As the train pulled out of the station and reached a speed of about ten miles an hour, the missionaries dashed off the platform after the moving train. Running until they could get hold of the hand rails on the passenger cars, they swung their luggage and themselves onto the train.

They didn't think the conductor would put them off going at full speed. And he would not halt the train on their account.

They were wrong. At the next town, the engineer stopped the train. The conductor ordered them off. They were picked up by the military police and interrogated.

Seibold produced the pass written by the Emmerich military police captain and the group was released.[15]

Back at the station, the missionaries were allowed to board a train going north to Osnabruck. All along the way, railroad crossings, bridges and factories were guarded by armed soldiers and anti-aircraft guns.

At Osnabruck, they were just minutes too late for a train that would have taken them directly to Hamburg.[16]

As with every station, the missionaries had been in during the previous thirty-six hours, the Osnabruck depot was filled with people. The weary young men stood on the crowded platform and wondered what to do next. Then someone suggested they find something to eat.

Although they had money for a substantial meal, they could find no one who would sell them more than a few rolls. They were told food had been put on high rations and the station vendors had been sold out for hours.[17]

As the eight waited in the station, they were joined by six other West German missionaries who had just come from Bentheim. Ben Lasrich, Donald Poulton, Louis Haws, Claytor Larsen, Frank Knutti and Ellis Rasmussen.

One of the group asked a station official when the next train was due.

The man frowned and shook his head. "No trains for several hours," he replied.

A few minutes later an unexpected north-bound train arrived.[18] Since they did not know how quickly the train would depart, the missionaries wasted little time getting aboard. Two of them climbed into a car and lowered the window. Outside, the others pitched their luggage through the open window. Then as the train began moving forward, the missionaries jumped aboard.[19]

In Bremen, the missionaries were once more "bumped off" to make room for soldiers. In that station, they assigned one missionary to watch for incoming trains while the remaining men tried to rest on the wooden benches in the waiting room.

Train after train come into the depot but the missionaries were refused passage on each of them. At last, they decided they must change their own luck.

Just as in Munster, when the next north-bound train left the station, they raced after it, threw their luggage aboard and vaulted into the moving train. And just as in Munster, they were put off at the next stop.

They appointed a sentry to watch for incoming trains, while the others rested on the benches in the station. They were allowed passage on the next train going to Hamburg. Again, two of them rushed onto the train and opened the windows while the others quickly passed their luggage into the car and then boarded on the run.

They arrived in Hamburg at 11:00 p.m., just three minutes too late to catch a train that would have taken them directly to Copenhagen via the ferry.

Ellis Rasmussen approached the station master and asked if he knew when the next north-bound train was due.

"No trains," the station master replied brusquely.

"There has to be a train, "Rasmussen insisted.

The station master shook his head. "No trains!"

"But there has to be!"

"There aren't any trains for you. Now or any time. They are all being used for troop transport!"

"There has to be a train! We have to get out of the country."

In exasperation the man replied. "It would be easier to buy a ticket and sail to America!"

About that time, someone in the station told the missionaries there was a train headed for points north which was due to arrive shortly in the nearby town of Altona.[20]

They rushed to Altona and boarded the north-bound train at 1:30 a.m. Two hours later they arrived in Neumuster where they were again "bumped off".

In that station, they were able to buy some knackwurst soup. Then, exhausted, they put their heads down on the tables in the waiting room and tried to sleep.[21, 22]

ENDNOTES

1 Richard D. Poll interview.

2 John W. Dean account.

3 Poll interview, Dean's account and written accounts by Meyer, Loertscher and Kratzer. Also Horsley personal interview.

4 Smith, Joseph Fielding, "Border Incident," op cite.

5 Grace Olsen Ensign interview. Arnold Hildebrandt tape.

J. Richard Barnes also supplied additional information in a tape recorded account.

6 Reconstructed from accounts by Louis Haws, Ellis Rasmussen's article, "Border Incident: Inside Germany", mission journal of Ben Lasrich and Frank Knutti interview.

7 Kest, John Robert. "Border Incident: Inside Holland", *The Improvement Era* (Dec. 1943, pp.753-3,793)

8 Reconstructed using article by Rasmussen and information from Lasrich and Haws.

9 Ferryle McOmber letter and information from Norman Seibold.

10 Neither Vern Marrott nor William Manning can explain what happened at Zevenaar, Holland. All the missionaries with him had the same amount of money and all had "through tickets". But only Marrott and the Rieglers were allowed to cross the border. Manning and Griner were told no refugees were being admitted.

11 Marrott tape recording, William Manning letter, Grant Baker interview, and written accounts from Owen Ken Earl and Charles Jenkins, Jr.

12 Seibold interview. McOmber letter. Jenkins and Earl accounts. Baker interview.

13 Earl interview

14 Baker interview.

15 Jenkins account.

16 Earl account.

17 Baker interview.

18 Haws letter.

19 McOmber letter.

20 Knutti interview. Ellis Rasmussen article in Improvement Era.

21 Earl account.

22 Missionaries involved in this incident were Norman Seibold, Ferryle McOmber, Dean Griner, William Manning, Grant Baker, Owen Ken Earl, Charles Jenkins, Jr., Alfred Alder, Ellis T. Rasmussen, Frank Knutti, Ben Lasrich, Donald Poulton, Claytor Larsen and Louis J. Haws.

—FOUR—

MONDAY, 28 AUGUST 1939

Sanctuary

Fourteen Missionaries Cross into Denmark.

(Norman Seibold, Ferryle McOmber, Dean Griner, William Manning, Grant Baker, Owen Ken Earl, Alfred Alder, Charles Jenkins, Jr., Ben Lasrich, Donald Poulton, Louis J. Haws, Claytor Larsen, Frank Knutti and Ellis T. Rasmussen.)

In Neumunster, the fourteen missionaries spent a short and uncomfortable night on the wooden benches and tables in the railway station.

That morning, they learned a train, destined for Kiel, was due in the depot. The station agents felt there was a good chance they would be granted passage on it.

Having neither bathed nor shaved in three days and anticipating their arrival in Denmark sometime that afternoon, all the missionaries cleaned up as best as they could.

At 8:00 a.m. the train pulled into the station and the young men squeezed into the already-packed cars.

They waited and waited but there was no sign that the train would be departing anytime soon. Although it was still morning, the overcrowded cars were stuffy and uncomfortably warm. The passengers lowered the windows.

After an hour, another train pulled into the depot and stopped next to the one on which the missionaries waited. Its windows were also open and one of the young men suggested they "transfer".

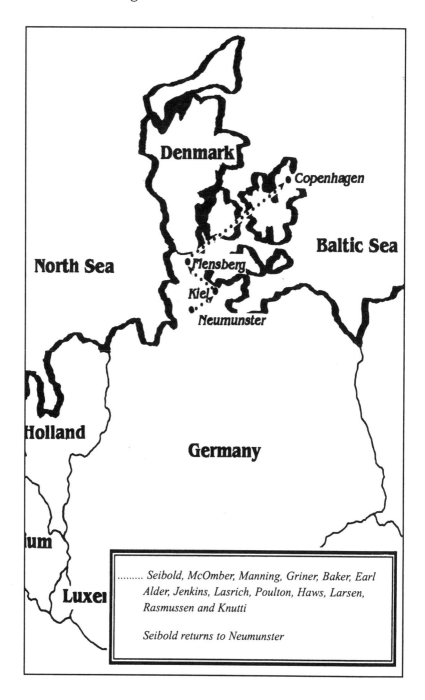

Denmark

Copenhagen

Baltic Sea

North Sea

Flensberg

Kiel

Neumunster

Holland

Germany

Luxer

.... *Seibold, McOmber, Manning, Griner, Baker, Earl
Alder, Jenkins, Lasrich, Poulton, Haws, Larsen,
Rasmussen and Knutti*

Seibold returns to Neumunster

They climbed through the windows of their train and in through the windows of the second one. Having no more than found seats, the train into which they had just climbed began to move. Within minutes was on its way to Kiel.

While they rode, Frank Knutti struck up a conversation with a Jewish boy. The child told Knutti that his family had been turned away by all of Germany's border neighbors. Denmark was their last hope. There was nowhere else for them to go.

In Kiel, where the missionaries were to change trains again, they employed their usual method of boarding. Two of them climbed into the train while the others remained on the platform to pitch all their luggage through the open windows.

A physically strong young man, Norman Seibold was considered the missionaries' best "pitcher". Unfortunately, Seibold failed to notice that the two missionaries who boarded the train had not yet lowered the window. The suitcase flew through the air and crashed into the thick glass, shattering it.

In stunned silence, they stared at the glass on the platform. If the conductor discovered the broken window, he would turn them over to the military police and there would be another long delay.

Fortunately, the conductor was at the opposite end of the train. He had not seen the accident. Thinking quickly, the missionaries on the platform kicked the glass under the train and onto the railroad tracks. Then the missionaries inside the compartment carefully lowered what was left of the shattered window so that none of the glass spears were visible.

All but two of the missionaries from the platform jumped into the cars. The conductor glanced down the length of the train to see that all passengers were aboard. The two waved and shouted, "Fertig! Fertig!" (Ready!)

The conductor hesitated for just a few seconds, then signaled the engineer to proceed.[1]

It was just a bit after noon when the Denmark-bound missionaries arrived in Flensburg, a city on the German-Danish border.[2]

The Gestapo scrutinized their passports and searched their belongings. They demanded to see their cameras. The officers opened the cameras and exposed the film.

Ferryle McOmber experienced a tense moment at the check point. The year before, he had purchased a Kodak Cine 8mm movie camera. Then, as he and the other missionaries fled across Germany, he photographed the surrounding county side. Inadvertently he also photographed a column of military trucks and several stationary anti-aircraft guns.

One peculiarity of the camera saved McOmber's film. The camera used 16mm film, but ran it through twice and exposed only one-half of the width at a time. When one side of the film had been exposed, McOmber turned it over and put it back in the camera. The dial then read "full", meaning it was loaded with unexposed film.

With a nonchalance he did not feel, McOmber approached the officer at the check point where the blackshirt demanded to see his camera. The missionary produced it.

"Is there film in the camera?"

"Yes," said McOmber. "I have just loaded it."

When the officer expressed his doubt, McOmber made a display of pointing out the dial which read, "full". "Even I," said McOmber in a loud, critical voice, "who have been in Germany only a few months can read a camera dial."

The blackshirt's face reddened and he glanced at the group of people who had collected at the check point. "Okay," he answered tersely, "get out of here."

McOmber slipped through the check point with his camera and film intact. He quickly lost himself in the crowd on the other side.[3]

The missionaries arrived in Padborg, a Danish border town, at 1:00 p.m. that afternoon. They had spent three days traveling across Germany in hot, overcrowded railway cars rarely having the comfort of a seat. They had slept only minutes at a time on benches and tables and floors in various railway stations. And they had had almost nothing to eat.

They had been arrested, interrogated and threatened on several occasions and put off trains more than a dozen times.

For those exhausted missionaries, the Danish language sounded like music and the peaceful countryside seemed like Heaven.

Seibold Returns to Germany

In the border town of Padborg, Denmark, Norman Seibold wired President M. Douglas Wood in Copenhagen and informed him of the missionaries' safe arrival. He saw his thirteen fellow Elders onto a train bound for Copenhagen, and then, because he could not be certain he had found all the "lost" missionaries, Seibold boarded a south-bound train and headed back into Germany.

As the train stopped in German cities, towns and villages along the Dutch border, Seibold got off and, whistling the mission song, searched the railway stations in vain. He found no more stranded missionaries.

In the Neumunster depot, Seibold walked restlessly up and down the platform. A silent but clear urging from within took him out of the station and into the street. Then down another street and around a corner. He stopped in front of a gasthaus—a pub.

It wasn't the sort of place a missionary was likely to frequent. However, the unmistakable feeling became stronger. He should go in. Seibold thought about his father and how his father would feel if he knew Seibold had gone into the gasthaus. But the feeling was so strong it propelled the missionary through the door.

There, seated at a table were two young men in dark suits and white shirts.

There was no doubt about their identities. One of them glanced up at the door. Surprise, then relief flooded his face. He came out of his chair with a bound, his hand outstretched.

"Am I ever glad to see you," he said and pumped Seibold's hand up and down.

"I'll never forget the look in that man's eyes," Seibold later recorded.

The two stranded missionaries had found their way to the gasthaus, exhausted and hungry and spent the last of their money on fruit juice. Until Seibold came through the door, they had no idea what they should do or where they should go.

Seibold gave the pair two tickets to Copenhagen and enough money for a decent meal. Then he saw them onto a Denmark-bound train.[4]

Vern Marrott and the Rieglers

Through the morning of Monday, August 28, Vern Marrott and the Rieglers rode to the safety of the Hague, Holland. President Murdock greeted them warmly in the mission office and treated them to a meal of beans and bread. White bread, at that, with absolutely no trace of sawdust or wood splinters. Best of all, however, was dessert. Ice cream with real pineapple.

After they had eaten, President Murdock instructed them to travel to nearby Rotterdam where an orientation in the branch meeting house was being held for all refugee missionaries.

When Marrott and the Rieglers had been turned back at the Dutch border the day before, their trunks, having been checked to Rotterdam, were sent into Holland without them. The missionaries decided while they were in Rotterdam they would pick up their luggage at the station.

Marrott cautioned the Rieglers if there should be any difficulty, he would be the spokesman. He reminded them they did not have permission from the Dutch government to be in Rotterdam and the couple's obvious German accents would surely attract suspicion.

In the Rotterdam depot, they discovered their trunks had been sent to another railway station in the city. On the way to the other station, the three became lost. Forgetting herself in her anxiety, Sister Riegler approached a Dutch policeman and, in German, asked for directions.

Immediately, the officer arrested the three as German spies and took them to the police station.

The officers separated the missionaries and thoroughly questioned each of them. Then the police brought the three back together. They reminded Marrott and the Rieglers they were being charged with espionage and conducted the trio to the office of Rotterdam's Chief of Police.

Marrott and the Rieglers were convinced they were about to receive a prison sentence, or worse.

Instead, the police chief asked, "Do you know a Mr. so and so in Salt Lake City?"

The missionaries replied that they did not know him.

"He was on the police force here in Rotterdam. He joined your Church several years ago and now lives in Salt Lake City. I thought you might know him."

Again, the missionaries replied that they did not know the man.

"I've known many Mormons in the city over the years," he continued. "I know the branch president here. I'll telephone him and have him come and get you."

Surprised, but nonetheless relieved, the missionaries thanked the police chief and were released into the custody of the Danish branch president.[5]

Seibold Continues His Search

Norman Seibold did not go into Denmark on that August 28th. Unaware that all the West German missionaries who had been stranded on the Dutch border were safely out of Germany, he continued his search for another twenty-four hours.

For the lone, weary Elder, that twenty-four hours stretched beyond measurement as he rode the overcrowded trains, without sleep and little to eat. At last, prompted that he had fulfilled the responsibility he had accepted, he returned to the Danish border on Tuesday, August 29.

When Seibold arrived in Copenhagen, President Wood threw his arms around the young man in a mixture of relief, gratitude and joy.[6]

On Friday, 1 September 1939, the Nazis marched into Poland and the war everyone predicted became a reality.

On Sunday, 3 September, Great Britain declared war on Germany. Within hours, France followed suit and that same day shots were fired over the Rhine River.

ENDNOTES

1 This account was reconstructed using information from letters written by Own Ken Earl, Louis J. Haws, Charles Jenkins, Jr., William Manning and Ferryle McOmber. Additional information was supplied in personal interviews with Frank Knutti and Norman Seibold. Also from The Improvement Era article by Ellis T. Rasmussen and the mission journal of Ben Lasrich.

2 It is interesting that Ben Lasrich and Donald Poulton, who were originally assigned to the city of Flensburg, should travel across Germany to the Dutch border then back across Germany to the city of Flensburg where they passed into Denmark.

3 McOmber letter.

4 Seibold interview.

5 Tape recording by Vern Marrott.

6 Forty-five years after the evacuation, Norman Seibold was to comment that when he gets in a large crowd, he still looks for lost missionaries.

—FIVE—

IN COUNTRIES OF REFUGE

In Switzerland

Six West German missionaries escaped Germany to Switzerland. For four of these, assigned to cities in southern Germany, the evacuation was simply a matter of crossing the Swiss border.

Two of the Elders, however had a different experience.

During that August of 1939, Nephi Henry Duersch and his companion, Robert J. Gillespie, were laboring in a rural area around the small towns of Frankenburg and Haag, Austria.

Because of the isolation of the area, the two missionaries were unaware of the growing tension in Germany.

When the evacuation telegrams went out on August 25, Duersch and Gillispies were bicycling from one Austrian village to another, visiting members and teaching where invited.

The mission office staff waited in vain to receive their departure telegram with the code word "Quickmere". They sent additional messages by wire and telephone but all went unanswered.

As the staff prepared to leave Frankfurt, President Wood instructed the German women who worked as secretaries and bookkeepers to continue their attempts to reach the pair.

They were unsuccessful until September 2, nine days after the first evacuation telegrams were sent. Duersch and Gillespie had just returned to their apartment in Frankenburg and were surprised to receive a message to call the mission office.

When they did, one of the German women in the office told them that President Wood and all the missionaries had left the country. She instructed them to go to a neutral country as quickly as possible.

Since Holland had closed its borders and Denmark was too far away, they knew their only hope was Switzerland. They packed, gave their bicycles to a German family and raced to the railway station. They hoped to catch a train to Stuttgart, Germany, where they might find a train bound for Basel, Switzerland. Duersch and Gillespie arrived at the depot just as a west-bound train, which happened to be two hours late, pulled into the station.

Although the station was a bedlam of frantic confusion, the missionaries managed to get tickets and squeeze into one of the cars. As it stopped in cities and towns along the route, a few people, mostly soldiers reporting to their units and vacationers returning home, got off the train. But many more people jammed into it.

Several times during that trip, their train was pulled off its tracks while troop trains passed. The Elders were never sure when or if the train would continue.

Every depot stop was the same. Great crowds of people fought to board the already loaded cars. Pushing and shoving, more and more people forced their way into the cars. Fear, almost tangible, hung in the air.

In an effort to relieve the tension, Duersch took out his harmonica and began to play a tune. A distraught German in the same car broke into an angry tirade.

"This is no time for happy music!" he shouted.

Duersch put away his harmonica.

When they arrived in Stuttgart, the missionaries learned that a train for Switzerland was due to depart the station in a matter of minutes. They hurried to another platform and boarded that train.

They crossed the Swiss border, arriving in Basel at 2:00 a.m. Mission President Thomas E. McKay found a place for them to sleep in the home of a Church member. Two hours later they learned that the Swiss border had just been closed to refugees.

The next day, September 3, the Germans and French were firing at each other over the Rhine River.[1]

Two other pairs of missionaries also made their way to Switzerland. They were Sylvan Burgi and Willard Doxey along with Elmer Stettler and his companion, Doris Black.

All six missionaries who had gone to Switzerland were assigned to work with the Swiss missionaries. After several weeks, they received instructions to return to the United States.

They were told to leave by ship from Bordeaux, France. As they crossed that country by train, there were repeatedly bumped off. Since the trains were no longer running according to schedule in France, the Elders frequently had to wait for hours before getting passage on another one. The trip to Bordeaux, which should have taken nine or ten hours, took them two and a half days.

At last, in Bordeaux, the missionaries boarded their ship during a blackout and sailed for New York and home.[2]

In Hungary

Warren Kirk had been released from the West German Mission and was traveling through Europe when the evacuation telegrams went out.

One night, while he slept in a Hungarian hotel, a telephone call came for him. It was a missionary in the Frankfurt office telling him about the evacuation order. He was told that they had had a great deal of difficulty locating him and had been telephoning every city and hotel they could think of where he might be staying. He told Kirk, "We'll be out of here by ten o'clock tomorrow morning. You'd better leave, too."

Kirk crossed Hungary and Austria by train. In Germany, he was bumped off but found transportation by Post Wagon or bus where, he said, he became intimately acquainted with fleas and lice.

Later, he was fortunate to find and board an over-crowded train for Frankfurt. Unfortunately, he did not have a ticket for that destination and he worried that he would be put off.

"Don't worry about it," a German woman in the same compartment told him. "The train is so crowded, the conductor won't bother to check tickets."

As Kirk and the woman talked, the conversation turned to war. She told him matter-of-factly, "I lived through the last one. But I have a doctor friend who will ensure that I won't have to live through this one." She lowered her voice, "I have a black pill."

In Frankfurt, Kirk went to the mission office.

The German women who worked there told him to continue north. They gave him the telephone number of a member in Hamburg. "You can stay there tonight," they told him.

He did so without incident and the next morning caught a train from Hamburg to Copenhagen.[3]

The Smiths in Denmark

Apostle Smith's presence in Copenhagen was to have a profound effect on many of the evacuated missionaries. One that lasted throughout their lives.

President and Sister Smith with evacuated Elders

Missionaries evacuated from the West and East German Missions pose with Joseph Fielding and Jessie Evans Smith and the Mission Presidents and their families in Copenhagen.

Each morning, the missionaries gathered at the chapel in the Danish Mission Home. There, they heard the political news of the day and held a special meeting, presided over by Apostle Smith.

During those meetings, Smith encouraged the missionaries to ask him gospel questions. He instructed them on many points of doctrine. Frequently, he turned to his scriptures and said, "Let's see what the Lord says about that...."

Many missionaries claimed they learned more about the gospel in those few days in Copenhagen than they had on their entire missions.

During that time, it was reported that Smith made several predictions. One of them about Denmark itself. He is reported to have said that because Denmark sheltered the missionaries during that crisis, it would not suffer the hardships of coming war in the same ways other European countries would. The predictions proved to be correct.[4]

In Denmark

For the first few days of their evacuation, the missionaries hoped they would be returning to Germany to finish their missions. As the days went by, however, it became increasingly obvious that the Polish crisis would not pass as quickly as the Czech crisis had a year earlier.

While they waited, the missionaries enjoyed sightseeing, swimming and, most of all, eating food they had rarely seen in Germany. Milk, butter, cheese, ice cream, whipping cream piled high on pastries and pies, fresh fruit, crisp vegetables, white bread and eggs with bacon or ham. There seemed to be so much good food, the missionaries ate until they thought they would burst.

Some of the missionaries got together and formed musical groups, performing original numbers at the daily meetings.

Copenhagen—31 August 1939
by John Dean and Harold Kratzer[5]
Tune: "Hand Me Down My Walking Cane"

Copenhagen, here we are
We came in from near and far,
If you want the inside dope
Oskar[6] took a German vote
Danzig wollte Heim ins Reich.[7]

So just like September last[8]
Telegrams went flying fast.
"Pack your trunks and rush away,
Train connections stop today."
All our hopes went flying away.

Prexies[9] feared we'd not get out
But to us there was no doubt.

In Copehnhagen: The Garffs, Woods, Toronto (Czech Mission President), Smiths

Workers sandbagging a museum in Copenhagen

All the boys were on their trunks,
They'd been there for months and months,
Half of them were schon[10] underway.

Some were sent to Netherlands
But we were offered no glad hands;
Kindest words were "About face!"
But the trunks went right on their way[11]

With no cash and little hope
We all landed here in Cope.
Good ice cream soon took our eye,
We eat so much we nearly die,
Thirty Kronen lasts just one day.

Besides food, another commodity in scarce supply in Germany had been uncensored news. The missionaries were as eager for that as they were the good food.

They learned about the Polish invasion and the declaration of war by England and France. They learned the German people were not told their country was officially at war with two other nations.

They also leaned that German U-boats sank an English ship carrying fourteen hundred passengers. More than two hundred of them were Americans.[12]

On Thursday, September 5, during the morning meeting, Apostle Smith announced the opening song for their devotional. It was the missionary anthem, "It May Not Be on a Mountain Height". At that moment, the missionaries knew they would not be going back to Germany.[13]

Smith announced that missionaries who had been out more than two years would be released and sent home.[14] Those who had served less than six months would be transferred to missions in Denmark, Norway and Sweden.

Many missionaries were shocked and saddened. Brokenhearted, Arnold Hildebrandt, who was to be sent back to the States, went to Apostle Smith and asked if there was any way he would be allowed to finish his mission in Europe.

Smith said, "Let me see what I can do."

Several hours later, Smith took Hildebrandt aside and put his arm around him. He said he had thought the matter over but he felt it best that Hildebrandt return to the United States. "Elder Hildebrandt, we will all be leaving soon," he said.[15]

The younger Elders were set apart as Danish, Swedish and Norwegian missionaries. However, within hours Elder Smith received word that Norway and Sweden had also closed their borders. The Elders would not be allowed entry into those countries.

There was nothing left to do but wait for ships to take the missionaries back home to the United States. Unfortunately, Denmark was crowded with American tourists also clamoring for sea passage home.

One group of missionaries was granted passage on a freighter, the S.S. Mormachawk, on September 5. More missionaries boarded the freighter S.S. Scanyork the following day. Another group did not get passage until September 11th.

A handful of missionaries, those reassigned to Denmark, were left behind. President Wood and his family were reassigned to Sweden in order to help close the mission there.[16]

In the Land Where the Hakenreuz Flies[17]
by John Dean and Harold Kratzer
Tune: "In the Shade of the Old Apple Tree."

President Garff, to your wife and you
We give our thanks for all that you do
And how grateful we are
That from Holland so far
Our Apostle and Sister Smith flew.
He can answer all questions that show
There's no gospel that he doesn't know
And through her lovely song[18]
We'll be carried along
Such a pleasure for me and for you.

Last year (1938) we sang in Holland...

We'll go back where the Hakenkreuz flies,
Where there ain't no ice cream, cake or pies.
Where the boys lose their hair
And the gals cease to care[19]
And we're scratching with tears in our eyes.[20]
We'll go tracting from morn until night
And we'll win friends with all of our might,
We'll eat black bread and thirst
We'll even stand the wurst
In the land where the Hakenkreuz flies.

But this year in Copenhagen (1939) we sing...

To the Hakenkreuz we've said goodbye
To return where the stars and stripes fly.
There's no wood in the bread,
And the dictators are dead,
And "Heil Hitler" is not praised on high.
They are sending us back to the States

By battleship, steamship or freight.
But if our choice were free
Missionaries we'd be
In the land where the Hakenkreuz flies![21]

In Holland

Fifteen West German missionaries managed, by various methods, to cross the German-Dutch border into Holland. Many of these were successful because they carried not only the ten German marks allowed them by law, but also some American currency and British visas. Others were successful because they took advantage of unusual situations and relied on their own ingenuity.

Two missionaries, George Peter Kuhn and Reed Oldroyd, were laboring in the city of Mannheim when they received the evacuation telegram of August 25. On the following day, when they were preparing to leave, a courier arrived from the post office. He delivered a message instructing them to telephone the mission office in Frankfurt. When they did so, they were told that the Dutch border had been closed to those who did not have extra money and a British visa or "through tickets". The young men were advised to go to the nearest Dutch Consulate and get visas before proceeding to Holland.

Since the closest consulate was in Frankfurt, they took a train to that city. When they arrived they found the doors of the two-story mansion locked.

They knocked and waited but no one came. Again they knocked, again there was no response. Because they could hear voices coming from inside the building, they walked around to the side door and knocked again. Still no answer.

At last, the pair began shouting and pounding on the door. The noise brought a consulate official to an upstairs window. "What do you want?" he called down to them.

"We're American citizens, and we need visas to get out of the country."

"All right, all right. Just a moment." The official came down and opened the door.

Inside the building the Elders were surprised to see that every room, every space was filled with somber-faced people. Hundreds of them. All wore the six-pointed Star of David pinned to their clothes.

The official found seats for the pair and brought them the appropriate papers to fill out and sign. Within moments they were granted their visas.

Two young Jewish women, both visibly upset, approached the two Americans and weeping, begged for help. They, like everyone else in the consulate, were attempting to leave Germany but had been denied visas.

Powerless, the Elders could do nothing to help the young women.

The missionaries returned to the railway station and boarded a train for Holland and safety.

Their train crossed the Dutch border somewhere near the Maas River. After the border officials scrutinized their papers, they allowed them to enter Holland. Their luggage, however, was held at the check point for several days before the missionaries were allowed to claim it.[22]

As Fred (Fritz) Duehlmeier and Dwayne Ward stood in the check point line at the Dutch border, a man, whom they assumed to be a railway official, beckoned to them. They left the line and followed him. Not a word was exchanged between them as he took them through a back passage which went around the check point to a waiting train. The two missionaries climbed on the train and minutes later were on their way to Rotterdam, despite the fact that they had no money, no 'through tickets' to London and no British visas. They never learned the identity of their benefactor in the Dutch railway station.[23]

Clark Hillam and Walter Welti entered Holland without the help or hindrance of legal procedures. When the pair arrived at the Dutch border, they were dismayed to find a long line of people at the check point. The line not only coiled around inside the building

Saturday, 2 Sept. 1939, in front of the Holland Mission Office.

1st row: Wesche, Hillam, Kuhn, Duehlmeier
2nd row: Buehner, Oldroyd, Goold, Marrott, John Robert Kest
3rd row: Kunkel, Ward, Rosenhan, Wimmer, Wells, Welti

but snaked outside and down the walkway as well. Everyone in Germany, it seemed, was trying to get out.

The missionaries went to the end of the line and waited. And waited. The line grew longer and seemed to be moving slower all the time. The Elders noticed many people being refused entrance to Holland. At last, Hillam told his companion, "We have train tickets. Let's go get on the train."

They left their place in line, walked out of the check point building and to a low fence that separated them from the train yard. On the other side stood a waiting train.

Despite the long line of people outside the check point building, the pair was unobserved as they stepped over the fence, crossed the yard and climbed into the back of the train. Within minutes the train pulled out of the station and headed for Rotterdam.

On that trip, no one bothered to check the missionaries' tickets or papers.[24]

In Rotterdam, Franklin J. Murdock, president of the Dutch Mission, made arrangements to accommodate the fourteen West German missionaries as well as Vern Marrott and the Rieglers.

It was obvious to him, however, that the ailing Rieglers were unable to deal with the physical and emotional stresses they had experienced during the evacuation. As quickly as passage could be booked on a ship departing for the United States, the Rieglers were returned to their home in Utah.[25]

The remaining fifteen missionaries waited in Holland. President Murdock assigned Erma Rosenhan to stay with two sister missionaries who were working in The Hague.[26] The fourteen Elders were sent to a youth hostel in Rotterdam.[27]

Because of the unstable situation in Germany, no one was certain whether the West German missionaries would be returning to their mission or if they would be reassigned to other missions in Europe. In the meantime, all they could do was wait.

In Rotterdam, the lives of the missionaries settled down to a routine. They breakfasted on hot chocolate and fruit at the youth hostel, then attended a devotional meeting held at a local branch building. In those daily meetings, they prayed and sang together, delivered and heard speeches on points of doctrine and discussed spiritual topics.

Following the meetings, the Elders took their meals with various Dutch member families as a cost of thirty five cents per meal. These meals consisted mostly of beans, cheese, bread and fresh fruits and vegetables which the missionaries considered a great treat after their experiences in Germany. One of the most commonly served dishes was a combination of french fried potatoes and dill pickles. The Elders ate ice cream until they thought they would be sick.

The afternoons belonged to the missionaries and the Church provided them with two guilders a day for spending money. President Murdock cautioned them, however, that the Dutch, remembering the tragedy of the last war, were antagonistic toward refugees. They were to keep a low profile when in the city and do absolutely nothing to call attention to themselves.

The missionaries found several ways to keep themselves busy. In discreet numbers of two or three, they went sight-seeing around Rotterdam. They kept their journals and wrote letters home, reassuring their families that they were safe.

Besides the missionaries, there were several other American men in the youth hostel and the group frequently played softball and football during the afternoons. In the evenings, the Elders once again had their meals with Dutch members. Then, to pass a few hours, some went to the English speaking movies. They saw "That Certain Age", "Going Places", "The Oklahoma Kid", and "Dawn Patrol". One of the missionaries described "Dawn Patrol" in his journal with a weary sadness as "a war movie".[28]

For a time, there was some discussion of sending the West German missionaries to Denmark. Means of transporting them could not be found, however. Going overland, through Germany was out of the question as was shipboard travel through the North and Baltic Seas. The Nazis had mined the seas and U-boat wolfpacks skulked the open waters. Many ships and their passengers and crews had already been torpedoed and lost. Alarmed, some

Dutch sailors had gone on strike, demanding more pay, better insurance and compensation for their families should a disaster occur.

Two young men from Missouri had been touring Europe when the Polish crisis began and managed to make their way to Rotterdam where they shared rooms in the hostel with the missionaries. The two booked passage on The Rhondo, one of the few ships leaving the Dutch ports for America.

About a week later, on September 19, the missionaries were surprised to find one of the Missourians had returned to the hostel. He told them The Rhondo had only been in the Atlantic a few hours when the crew mutinied and turned the ship toward another destination, traveling through unsafe waters. The two young men were eating lunch when the first explosion ripped through the ship. One of them ran up to the deck, the other went back to his cabin for his camera.

Within moments, The Rhondo hit a second mine and went down so quickly there was no time to release the life boats. Passengers and crew foundered helplessly in the water. Then someone discovered a life boat which had broken free of the sunken ship and was floating half full of water.

Several people managed to bail out the water and then paddle around picking up survivors. The Missourian who had gone up on deck when the first mine exploded was in the water for two and a half hours before the life boat rescued him.

Twenty of the thirty-seven passengers and crew crowded into the little vessel which was only built for ten. The overloaded boat tossed about in the ocean for fifty-nine hours before it was discovered by a passing ship.

The remaining seventeen people, including the Missourian who went for his camera, were lost. After recording the above story in his journal, George Wimmer joked, "Hope our boat doesn't sink." Then added, "It won't."[29]

All during this time, the missionaries heard unusual rumors from Germany. These tales reported that many Germans were rebelling against their Nazi leaders. Men refused to report to their military units. People began to decry Hitler and his regime openly.

Anti-Nazi posters appeared on public buildings. The Nazis took steps to snuff out the public rebellion. The stories stopped.

The missionaries began to realize the crisis was not going to end as soon as they had hoped. More and more, it looked as if they would not be returning to Germany nor the people they had come to love. Some entertained hopes they would be reassigned to other missions in Europe. However, they, too, were to be disappointed.

Word came from Apostle Joseph Fielding Smith in Copenhagen that all evacuated missionaries would return to the United States to serve the remainder of their missions.

Time and again, arrangements were made for the West German missionaries in Holland to depart. And time and again, they packed and unpacked as the arrangements fell through.

At last, on September 25, a full month after the evacuation, the missionaries climbed on a train to Antwerp, Belgium. In that city, they boarded the S.S. Pennland at 11:00 p.m. They stood on the deck and watched the lights on the shore fade and disappear as the ship steamed away from the port and into the open ocean.[30]

ENDNOTES

1 Letter from Robert J. Gillespie. Additional information came from an interview with Bertha Raisch Duersch. Sister Raisch was a German Saint working as a bookkeeper in the West German Mission Office at the time of the evacuation. After WWII, she came to the U.S. and married Nephi Henry Duersch.

2 Personal interview with Elmer Stettler. Sylvan Burgi letter.

3 Personal interview with Warren Kirk.

4 When the writer began hearing stories of the 1939 evacuation more than thirty years ago, they were always coupled with a reported Elder Smith prediction that Holland would suffer for turning the missionaries away. During the course of the research, however, none of the evacuated missionaries who were asked, said they could remember Smith making such a statement. But many did say it would come as no surprise if

he had. The fact is Holland, which prided itself on its long history of neutrality, was attacked by Germany on the first of May 1940 and fell within hours.

5 The songs written by Dean and Kratzer were supplied by Dean and verified by others.

6 "Oskar" was a name used for Hitler.

7 "Danzig desires to come home to the Reich."

8 Refers to the 1938 evacuation during the Czech crisis.

9 Mission presidents.

10 Already.

11 In their haste, it did not seem to matter to many of the evacuating missionaries that their trunks were left on their Holland bound trains while they were stopped at the border. Their luggage went on to Rotterdam while the missionaries ended up in Copenhagen with only the clothes on their backs.

President Murdock of the Dutch mission, had the presence of mind to round up all the trunks and then assign them to missionaries who were going home. Those missionaries took them back to the United States.

Erma Rosehan said she was nervous about taking Grant Baker's luggage through American customs. As a single woman, she was sure someone would be suspicious of her traveling with a trunk full of men's clothing.

Harold Kratzer and Richard Larkin Glade checked their trunks to Rotterdam then returned to their rooms where they found another telegram instructing them to go to Denmark instead of Holland. They hurried back to the station and discovered that the baggage handler, knowing that the Dutch border was closed, had taken their luggage and stored it, waiting for their return.

Others were not that fortunate. It was many months before luggage sent to Rotterdam eventually reached Elders reassigned to missions in the United States. Others finished their missions in borrowed clothes.

12 Written accounts by Jenkins and Manning.

13 George Blake letter.

14 Missionaries called to an English-speaking country served a two-year mission. However, because there was then no language training, a missionary called to a foreign mission was called for two and a half or three years.

15 Tape recording made by Arnold Hildebrandt.

16 Personal interview with Fred Duehlmeier.

17 The Hakenkreuz or Swastika was a symbol of the Third Reich and was the image on Germany's red flag.

18 Jesse Evans Smith was a member of the Tabernacle Choir.

19 Long standing joke—missionaries loose two things—hair and sweethearts.

20 Refers to the common problem West German missionaries had. Fleas.

21 Despite inconveniences, shortages and discomforts, most missionaries wanted to return to Germany and continue their missions there.

22 Interview with Kuhn and a letter from Oldroyd.

23 Duehlmeier interview.

24 Hillam interview.

25 Wimmer journal. Most of the information about the missionaries in Holland came from his journal.

26 Information from Rosenhan.

27 Kuhn interview.

28 Wimmer journal.

29 Wimmer journal and Rosenhan account.

30 Wimmer journal and Marrott tape.

—Six—

By Freighter to the U.S.A.

One of our Elders was asked if he was a bit anxious about going home on a freighter and being led out of Denmark by a German pilot through the mines. He said, "That is child's play after the things we have been through in getting out of Germany. I don't think, after all the trouble the Lord went to there, that he is going to let us drown in the middle of the ocean."

—M. Douglas Wood

The Mormachawk

In Copenhagen on September 5, 1939, Apostle Joseph Fielding Smith announced missionaries serving less than twenty-four

Missionaries watch as workers paint a U.S. flag on a freighter scheduled to carry them home.

Modeling makeshift life jackets are Kirk, Larsen, Blake, Knudsen, Dennett and Anderson (photo by George Blake)

months and more than six months would be sent back to the United States to finish their missions.

During that meeting, President Mark Garff of the Danish Mission read the names of those missionaries who were to leave that day on the Mormachawk, a freighter of the Moore-McCormick Lines.

The vessel, with accommodations for the crew and twelve tourists, had been partially converted to a passenger ship.

Instead of freight, cots were placed in the below-deck holds. One hundred and twenty-six passengers, including forty-five missionaries from the West and East German Missions, crowded aboard.

Ken Earl scouted the freighter's "facilities" and found they consisted of "one washroom for gents and one for ladies. In the gents room there is a shower, one wash bowl and one etc."

The Mormachawk was scheduled to sail at 5:00 p.m., but was held up while cork-filled life rafts were stacked on deck. The missionaries scheduled to leave later, were there to see the "lucky forty-five" off.[2]

Weilenman, Earl, Olsen, Robins, Hildebrandt & Wirthlin on the Mormachawk headed for the good old U.S.A.

Because Nazi U-boats patrolled the waters of the Baltic, the crew of the Mormachawk painted huge American flags (America was still neutral) on the sides and deck of the ship.

There was still danger in crossing the Baltic Sea, however, the Nazis had planted mines in the waters. Fortunately for all on board, the Mormachawk had a German co-pilot to guide the ship through the mined areas.

It was smooth sailing between Copenhagen and Stavanger, Norway. While docked in Stavanger on September 7, the missionaries walked through parts of the city and dined on the good food available in its many shops.

All through the day and following night, cargo was being loaded onto the freighter. The cargo included fifteen head of cattle and three head of small Norwegian horses.

The livestock were stabled in a hold next to the one occupied by Ken Earl, Arnold Hildebrandt and several Elders from the East German Mission. The noise and odor drove the missionaries to the cold, windy, upper deck where they spent most of their time.

In an effort to avoid open waters and a possible confrontation with hostile vessels, the freighter sailed north to the coast of Iceland.

The seas became choppy and rough and, because the freighter was not as stable as an ocean liner, many passengers became seasick. Buckets were taken into the holds for those who were not strong enough to make it to the decks' railings. Many of the sick missionaries claimed they would have preferred being torpedoed to spending another hour on the Mormachawk.

The weather compounded the passengers' misery. Despite the season, it was cold and rainy. Those who were well enough to leave the malodorous hold, spent the days on the deck, wrapped in blankets. And some passengers stayed on deck all night rather than endure the stench down in the hold.[4]

During the night of September 10, the ship's engine malfunctioned and by the time it was repaired, the ship had been blown off course. But the following morning, the Mormachawk was under way again. The storm continued until September 14, when the ship reached the coast of Nova Scotia.

The Mormachawk plowed south and finally reached a peaceful haven when it docked in Portland, Maine on Saturday, September 16.

The missionaries had spent eleven days in an overcrowded freighter on rough, frigid seas, threatened by the possibility of mines and U-boats.

Ken Earl's journal for that date:

> Up at 4:30 a.m. and got packed, ready to get off. The City of Portland sent a fire boat out to welcome us. Shot sprays of water all over. Had a good breakfast. Docked at Pier #1 at 7:30 a.m. It took from then until 3:00 p.m. before all were through the customs and ready to go.
>
> There were a number of reporters there to get a story, but none of our group talked—except generally. The president of the First National Bank wanted the missionary group up for dinner as his guests. Couldn't be arranged.

Left at 3:00 p.m. for New York City on a special train for "refugees".

In New York City, those who were to be reassigned to missions in the United States met in the Manhattan Chapel with Apostle Joseph Fielding Smith. He had them sing, "I'll Go Where You Want Me to Go, Dear Lord", and then announced their new assignments.

The ScanYork

The S.S. Scanyork, a 6,000 ton freighter, was also converted to a passenger ship to transport sixty evacuated West and East German missionaries and one-hundred and fifty other Americans back to the United States.

Straw cots were crowded into the dank below-deck holds for the passengers. Additional "bathroom facilities" consisted of galvanized buckets.

American flags had been painted on the stern, the sides, and the hatches to identify the ship as a neutral one.

A mine sweeper accompanied the ship from the North Sea into the Atlantic Ocean. The next day, the passengers learned that the sweeper was destroyed by a mine on its return to Copenhagen.

On it's second day out of Copenhagen, the freighter sailed into rough seas and almost all the passengers became ill. More buckets were brought into the hold which was, by then, dubbed the "bear pit". Those who could escape the foul air spent their days and some of their nights on deck in spite of the icy Arctic winds.

Fourteen of the missionaries sought the warmth of the ship's lounge. When everyone else went to bed, they claimed couches and chairs and spent the remaining nights of the voyage there.

A few days out of port, the captain called the able passengers together. He explained that his crew, while performing their regular duties, also had the extra responsibility of watching for mines and hostile vessels. They were overworked and exhausted. He asked that some of the passengers volunteer in relieving the crews. The passengers agreed to do whatever the captain wanted them to do.

Some of the missionaries were assigned to the galley and had memorable experiences attempting to prepare and serve meals while the ship floundered in the stormy waters. Others worked in the offices of the ship's captain and doctor.

West German missionaries aboard the SS ScanYork

Leland Blatter and Calvin Bartholomew were assigned to the crow's nest. Wearing protective arctic clothing, they took turns climbing the topmost lookout and scanning the ocean through binoculars.

One day, a Nazi war vessel approached the ship. By radio, the German captain communicated with the captain of the ScanYork and then let the shipful of Americans pass unharmed. On September 9, Bartholomew sighted a British man o' war. With its huge guns trained point blank on the freighter, the captain demanded identification.

After the ScanYork provided credentials, the British crew searched the vessel. When they found no contraband, they allowed the ship to continue its' voyage.

A few days later, Blatter spotted a submarine. As the vessel came alongside, word spread through out the ship that they were being shadowed by a U-boat. Even the most ill of the passengers in the hold managed to stagger up on deck.

Frank Knutti, who suffered from appendicitis as well as sea sickness, struggled to join the rest. As he looked over the railing, he was disappointed to discover the submarine was not a U-boat but an English submarine. "I was so sick, I just wanted to die," he said.

Monday, September 18, dawned bright and clear. "Beautiful weather for landing," Donald Anderson recorded. After twelve days in the stormy north Atlantic, the ScanYork sailed into New York Harbor.[6]

The Mormacwren

The Mormacwren of the Moore-McCormick Lines, like the other ships to leave Copenhagen with missionaries aboard, was a freighter with accommodations for only a few passengers. Yet on this, its maiden voyage, it carried over two hundred fifty.

Because there were not adequate life boats for that many passengers, the ship had five large wooden rafts secured to the decks.

With huge American flags painted on its decks and sides, it set sail to Norway. Traveling at top speed, the captain thought if the ship struck a Nazi mine, the vessel would pass over it before the mine exploded.

Unfortunately, the speed took a toll on the new engines and one burned out before they reached Stavanger. The missionaries accepted "watch" duty as the ship continued at half speed through the mined waters.

They left Norway on September 20 and sailed into the waters of the open ocean. On the 21, the sea became rough, the waves so large that, as the ship pitched over the crests, the missionaries could see its' propellers spinning in the air. Most of the passengers became too ill to leave their beds.

On the 22, the Mormacwren was stopped and investigated by an English destroyer before it was allowed to proceed.

The 25 and 26 saw a storm unequaled in more than a century. The huge waves crashed over the decks as the vessel pitched and tossed. By the 27, however, the sea had calmed and on October 1, the Mormacwren docked in New Jersey.

The grateful passengers disembarked and the missionaries boarded a train to New York City where they were reassigned to missions in the United States.[7]

The ScanPenn

The ScanPenn was also a freighter, its cargo mostly fish. The crew emptied the hold and cleaned it, but the more than two hundred and fifty missionaries and Polish and German Jews on board were well aware of its previous cargo.

ScanPenn missionaries standing on makeshift life raft.

The passengers who crowded into the cold and unpleasant hold slept in triple decker bunk beds.

The Jews were also quartered there and, for some unknown reason, refused to go above board. They even cooked their meals in the hold. But the missionaries preferred to spend every moment they could in the fresh, although cold, Arctic air.

Among the crew of the ScanPenn was a Norwegian captain who piloted the ship through the mined waters between Denmark and Norway. A Swedish ship, the Gronitain, followed in the wake of the ScanPenn to also avoid the mines.

Tragically, a Nazi U-boat torpedoed the Swedish vessel. The missionaries stood on the deck of the ScanPenn and watched the red glow against the night sky as the Gronitain burned and sank.

In the open North Sea, the sky was gray and overcast. The ocean was not exceptionally rough but many passengers became seasick. Some missionaries thought the seasickness was aided by the large quantities soft boiled eggs served at meals.

Unlike the other ships, the ScanPenn had no contact with U-boats or British ships. On September 26, however, German patrol planes flew alongside the vessel, but allowed it to proceed with no incident.

The ScanPenn docked in Boston, Massachusetts on October 7 after sixteen days at sea.[8]

The Pennland

The S.S. Pennland was a Dutch steamer. When the missionaries who evacuated to Holland boarded it they saw the name "Holland" spelled in electric lights on the sides. Lights were also strung from the smoke stacks. The life boats had already been lowered to deck level. On board were five hundred passengers, three hundred more than the ship was equipped to carry.

An English navigator piloted the ship through the mined waters of the English Channel. The passengers saw, not only destroyers, but a network of barrage balloons on the British coastline. These

The SS Pennland docked on 6 October 1939 with these West German Missionaries aboard.

balloons were intended to snare enemy aircraft should they try to fly over the coastline.

Erma Rosenhan remembered the young woman assigned to share a small cabin with her. The woman was an American married to a German naval officer. When war was declared, he insisted she return to the United States. Rosenhan said, "She cried the first two days out."

Although the crossing was an uneventful one, the passengers were nonetheless anxious for their safe arrival and on October 6, gratefully disembarked in New York City.[9]

In the April conference of 1940, J. Reuben Clark of the First Presidency reported the following:

> On August 24, 1939, there were in the European missions 697 persons, of whom 611 were young men and 63 young women missionaries, the other 23 were mission presidents and families.
>
> The first group landed in New York September 7, and the last one November 6, 1939. They (the missionaries) returned in 23 ships, each of which had to be met and the missionaries transported to temporary quarters. Heavy baggage handled exceeded 1,500 pieces; there were more than 10,000 letters and other mailed parcels.
>
> Of the 674 missionaries, 414 Elders and 32 lady missionaries were reassigned, the rest released.
>
> The total cost of this service in handling all these missionaries and mission presidents and families—a total of 697 persons—was only $2,271.47. Or $3.26 per person, for landing, housing, feeding and transportation from ships to headquarters and from headquarters to trains.

ENDNOTES

1-5 The information concerning the voyage of the Mormachawk was reconstructed using accounts from a personal interview with Frederick Balli, written accounts by Owen Ken Earl from his journal, personal interview with Grace Olsen Ensign and tape recorded account by Arnold Hildebrandt.

6 The information concerning the voyage of the ScanYork was reconstructed using information from the following: Tape recorded account by Donald Anderson, personal interview with Grant Baker, letter by Calvin Bartholomew, excerpts from Leland Blatter's journal, written account from John W. Dean, interview with Woodrow C. Dennett, letter by Louis J. Haws, interview with Frank Knutti, letter by Lawrence J. Meyer, written account by Ferryle McOmber, interviews with Norman Seibold and a letter from Elmer Tueller.

7 This information came from a written account by Charles Jenkins, Jr.

8 The information concerning the voyage of the ScanPenn was reconstructed using information from a tape-recorded account by J. Richard Barnes, a letter by Joseph Loertscher, written account from William R. Manning and an interview with Richard D. Poll.

9 The information concerning the voyage of the Pennland came from a personal interview with Fred Duehlmeier, a written account by Erma Rosenhan and a conference address by President M. Douglas Wood published by the *Deseret News* Church Section on 15 June 1940.

—SEVEN—

EPILOGUE: THE WAR AND AFTER

Over the years some memories dim while others shine all the brighter. Many West German missionaries view their time in Germany with a brightness of emotion though many claim a dimming of recall. They speak of the goodness of the German people, the stalwartness of the Saints with whom they lived and worked and their own great love of teaching the gospel in the cities and towns where they were assigned. They speak of their gratitude for having been able to serve in Germany. And yet, the saddest, most bitter memory is the sharpest. That of having their missions in Germany come to such an abrupt end.

Most of them remember the evacuation with great sorrow. Despite the personal danger in which some found themselves, the food shortages and inconveniences, the West German missionaries did not want to leave Germany. And even while they waited in Switzerland, Holland and Denmark, they prayed for and waited for the day when they could go back. They were deeply disappointed to find they would not be returning.

Most finished their missions in the United States where they found satisfaction in preaching the gospel, formed lasting bonds with new companions and learned to love the people whom they taught. But the events that sent the West German missionaries headlong out of Germany were to continue to touch their lives for years to come.

During the years of WWII, all the missionaries served their country in some capacity or another. Some served on the home front, others in the Air Force, Army, Marines and Navy in far flung places in the Pacific, the Atlantic, Europe and Asia. Only one, Donald Poulton, died in that service during the bombing of Pearl Harbor.

Another, Leland Blatter, gave up his life rather than have to fight, and possibly kill, the German people he loved.

Blatter had enlisted in the Air Force and was stationed at Fort Douglas, Utah, in 1941. By that time, the country was talking of America's entry into the war. Blatter's unit was already preparing.

Blatter worried that his unit would be assigned to the European Theater and he would be called upon to fly bombing missions over Germany. He expressed his growing anxiety and dismay to his father. He said he did not know how he could bomb people to whom he had preached the gospel. His father had tried to comfort and reassure him, at one point telling him that something would happen to prevent his having to fly a bombing mission over Germany. Something did happen.

In September 1941, the Blatter family received a call in their home of Chinook, Montana. The message said Leland had become ill and a family member should come to Utah at once. Blatter's father borrowed a car but arrived too late. Leland died September 14, 1941. The autopsy results were inconclusive. The cause of death was cautiously attributed to a sudden, high fever and kidney failure.

The Blatter family believed Leland's death was a fulfillment of his father's prophecy. They found comfort in believing Leland's desire was granted.

Other West Germany missionaries who went back into Germany as soldiers speak of their experiences with difficulty. They are reluctant to relive the memories of bombing raids, artillery action and even hand-to-hand combat within the country where they had once taught the gospel.

One former missionary, as a soldier, searched among the bodies of Germans killed during his unit's action, looking for members and investigators he had known while he was a missionary.

Some of those dreadful memories are edged with surprise and relief.

Former mission secretary J. Richard Barnes belonged to a unit that entered Frankfurt at the close of the war. One of the first things he did in Frankfurt was to go to the West German Mission Office. To his relief, he found the building still standing. It had sustained some damage in the shelling, but was in a condition to house several German member families who had lost their homes. He also said he found some of the belongings he had had to abandon during the evacuation.

In early 1945, while stationed near Dijon, France, Major Ken Earl, drove a jeep from Dijon to Frankfurt as soon as American troops liberated Frankfurt. He went to assess the damage to the mission office on Schaumain Kai Strasse.

He found an American Army Artillery Unit using it as its headquarters; sought and got permission of its commanding officer to go through the building and search for documents and records left by President Wood and the mission office staff. In his search, he found valuable records and correspondence—even letters he had written to President Wood while he was a missionary.

Earl boxed up all the records which appeared to warrant saving, took them with him back to Dijon and sent them to Church headquarters in Salt Lake City with an explanation.

After the war, two former missionaries married German girls.

Nephi Henry Duersch married Bertha Raisch, one of the women who worked in the mission office. They lived in Logan, Utah, until his death in 1974 and hers in 1988.

Geren Howell married German member Liselotte Heitele. The Heitele home in Stuttgart was frequently a gathering place for members. And the missionaries were sure to get a good meal there. As the missionaries were evacuating, some of the members, including Liselotte, went to the train station to see them off. Elder Howell asked Liselotte if he could write to her and she agreed.

Later, through the mail, when Geren proposed to Liselotte, she accepted. They wrote to each other until 1941 when the postal service between the two countries was discontinued. They had no word from, or of each other for the next four years.

Geren served in the Navy in the Pacific and Liselotte waited out the war in a crumbling Germany. Despite not knowing if the other had survived, Liselotte said she and Geren remained faithful to each other.

At the end of the war, and with the help of Church connections, Liselotte and Geren were able to locate each other and resume writing. At last, on 5 June 1947, Liselotte arrived in Salt Lake City and, after not seeing each other for eight years, she and Geren were married on June 10 by Elder Spencer W. Kimball.

During those years after the war, the former missionaries followed similar but separate paths. Families, educations and careers. Along the way, many have had great trials and sorrows and equally great triumphs and joy.

Many of them, though they went in different directions after their West German Mission experience, came back again to the blessings of missionary work and have sent their sons and daughters into the mission field. Some of those were sent to Germany. Many former West German missionaries have also returned to the mission field. Some more than once. J. Ralph Thompson managed four missions by the time of his death in 1987.

Even to this present day, the evacuation has had an impact on missionary work.

Here in the Idaho, Pocatello Mission, not all the missionaries have the luxury of cars. Many must depend on members for transportation. One Monday morning in May of 1999, this writer picked up Elders Carlos Zuniga and Douglas Zaug to take them to the laundromat.

On the way, Elder Zuniga told me he had read a talk by one of the general authorities about a mission evacuation from Nazi Germany. About how one missionary had traveled along the German-Dutch border looking for stranded missionaries and through inspiration had found many of them. He asked if I had heard about it.

I replied that I thought I knew something about it.

After the Elders finished their laundry, instead of taking them back to their house, I drove them the two miles to Norm Seibold's house.

The four of us sat and talked for twenty minutes or so. During those few minutes, Norm bore his testimony three times that the Lord takes care of his missionaries.

Elder Zuniga was particularly impressed with that testimony.

A month later, Elder Zuniga was contacted by the mission office and told he was being deported. After having served in the United States for a year, he was being returned to Chile. The reason for the deportation was not clear but a clerical error in the U.S. Immigration Office was the suspected cause.

Elder Zuniga was broken-hearted. All of us who knew Elder Zuniga were saddened.

While Elder Zuniga was waiting to be "processed" through Miami, he telephoned me. We talked for an hour about what had happened. The last thing he said to me was that meeting Norm Seibold and hearing his testimony was what sustained him through that trial.

Elder Zuniga was reassigned to the Chile Osorno Mission where his first assignment was to train branch presidents in that fast growing mission.

Standing back and looking at that incident now, I am humbled to realize it had been sixty years and Norm Seibold was still escorting missionaries.

Whatever the courses of their lives, the experiences of the missionaries who served in the West German Mission during the turbulent years of 1938 and 1939, and especially during that hot, humid August of their evacuation, have left upon them an influence so profound that it cannot be dimmed by memories that fade over the years.

Perhaps these missionaries have a sharper understanding of a missionary's love for the people he serves and teaches. An understanding of the desire to serve the Lord, no matter what the situation or how inconvenient and frustrating it may seem. An understanding of tolerance, of loving care for someone as a child of

God despite his country's political activities. An understanding of faith. That in serving the Lord he will literally send angels to bear up his servants.

On Saturday, 6 April 1940, former West German Mission President M. Douglas Wood bore his testimony in a conference talk titled, "The Lord Stood at Our Side". In that talk he said:

> I am grateful for this opportunity to bear you my testimony. I know that this is the true Church of God, that Jesus is the Christ, and that today Heber J. Grant is a prophet of our Father in Heaven. I am happy to have had this opportunity of working in Germany among the German people. I am happy to have had the privilege of being there during those hard times. The Lord stood at our side and never once did we want or were we unable to meet the situations at hand with His help.
>
> May we be generous in our judgments and tolerant toward all God's children, here in safety, in luxury, in our homes in the Land of the Free, is my humble prayer, and I ask it in Jesus' name. Amen.

BIBLIOGRAPHY

Ascherson, Neal. *World At War, Volume 1, A New Germany, 1933-39.* London: Thames Television, 1980 (Videotape)

Kest, John Robert. "Border Incident, Inside Holland," *The Improvement Era,* (Dec. 1943, pp793-4)

McCombs, Don and Worth, Fred L. *World War II: Strange and Interesting Facts,* New York: Greenwich House, 1983.

Rasmussen, Ellis T. "Border Incident, Inside Germany," *The Improvement Era,* (Dec. 1943, pp.752-3, 793)

Saloman, Henry and Hanser, Richard. *The Twisted Cross.* New York: NBC Television, 1980 (Videotape)

Schirer, William L. *The Nightmare Years.* Boston: Little, Brown and Co. 1984

Smith, Joseph Fielding. "Border Incident," *The Improvement Era,* (Dec. 1943, p. 752)

Speer, Albert. *Inside the Third Reich.* New York: MacMillan, 1970.

Unstead, R.J. *The Thirties.* Edinburgh: Morrison and Gibb, 1981

Wistrich, Robert. *Who's Who In Nazi Germany,* New York: Bonanza Books, 1982

Wood, M. Douglas. "The Lord Stood at Our Side," *Deseret News Church Section,* (15 June 1940)

PHOTOGRAPHIC GALLERY
(ALPHABETICAL LISTING)

Alfred William Alder
Donald R. Anderson
Grant W. Baker
J. Richard Barnes
John Bingham
Doris Black
George Blake
Leland Blatter
Grant Brown
Sylvan Burgi
John W. Dean
Woodrow Dennett
Willard B. Doxey
Fred H. Duehlmeier
Nephi Henry Duersch
Owen Ken Earl
Robert J. Gillespie
Adalbert and Elizabeth Goltz
William George Goold
Dean George Griner
Whitney D. Hammond
Louis J. Haws
Arnold Hildebrandt
Clark Hillam
A. Burt Horsley
Geren Howell
Charles Jenkins, Jr.
Warren Paul Kirk
Wesley P. Knudsen
Frank Knutti
Harold E. Kratzer
George P. Kuhn
Ben G. Lasrich

Robert Kunkel
Claytor Larsen
Joseph Loertscher
Howard W. Lyman
William R. Manning
Vern Marrott
Ferryle B. McOmber
Lawrence J. Meyer
Franklin J. Murdock (family)
Reed I. Oldroyd
Grace Olsen (Ensign)
Richard D. Poll
Stanford D. Poulson
Berta Raisch (Duersch)
Ellis T. Rasmussen
Katharine and Nikolaus Riegler
(barley coffee)
Erma Rosenhan
Elwood Scoville
Myron I. Seamons
Norman G. Seibold
Elmer E. Stettler
T. Frank Swallow
J. Ralph Thompson
Elmer R. Tueller
Dwayne Ward
Wilfred K. Wegener
John Wells
Edward J. Wirthlin
George Wimmer
Evelyn and M. Douglas Wood
Wilford Woolf

Alfred William Alder

Donald R. Anderson

Grant W. Baker

J. Richard Barnes

John Bingham

Doris Black

George Blake

Leland Blatter

Grant Brown

Sylvan Burgi

John W. Dean

Woodrow Dennett

Willard B. Doxey

Fred H. Duehlmeier

Nephi Henry Duersch

Owen Ken Earl

Robert J. Gillespie

Adalbert and Elizabeth Goltz

William George Goold

Dean George Griner

Whitney D. Hammond

Louis J. Haws

Arnold Hildebrandt

Clark Hillam

A. Burt Horsley

Geren Howell

Charles Jenkins, Jr.

Warren Paul Kirk

Wesley P. Knudsen

Frank Knutti

Harold E. Kratzer

George P. Kuhn

Robert Kunkel

Claytor Larsen

Ben G. Lasrich

Joseph Loertscher

Howard W. Lyman

William R. Manning

Vern Marrott

Ferryle B. McOmber

Lawrence J. Meyer

Franklin J. Murdock (family)

Reed I. Oldroyd

Grace Olsen (Ensign)

Richard D. Poll

Stanford D. Poulson

Berta Raisch (Duersch)

Ellis T. Rasmussen

Katharine and Nikolaus Riegler—barley coffee

Erma Rosenhan   Elwood Scoville

Myron I. Seamons

Norman G. Seibold

Elmer E. Stettler

T. Frank Swallow

J. Ralph Thompson

Elmer R. Tueller

Dwayne Ward

Wilfred K. Wegener

John Wells

Edward J. Wirthlin

George Wimmer

Evelyn and M. Douglas Wood

Wilford Woolf

BIOGRAPHY

Terry Bohle Montague is a BYU graduate and freelance writer, having written for newspapers, magazines, television, and radio. She is the published author of book length non-fiction and fiction. Her novel, *Fireweed*, the story of an LDS German family living in Nazi Berlin was inspired by the interviews she conducted during her research of *"mine angels round about"*.

She and her husband, Quinn, make their home in southern Idaho with a pair of Boston Terriers and several overweight cats. Their daughter, Elizabeth, and her husband, Leon Cazier live nearby.

INDEX